COMFORT
in the
STORM

May the Lord
always provide comfort
for you in the storms of
life! In Christ,
Janine Ridings

COMFORT
in the
STORM

DEVOTIONS *for the* CHEMICALLY SENSITIVE

JANINE RIDINGS

FOREWORD BY DAVID BUSCHER, M.D.

Pleasant Word

Packaged by Pleasant Word, PO Box 428, Enumclaw, WA 98022. The views expressed or implied in this work do not necessarily reflect those of Pleasant Word. The author(s) is ultimately responsible for the design, content and editorial accuracy of this work.

Unless otherwise noted, all Scriptures are taken from the Holy Bible, New International Version, Copyright © 1973, 1978, 1984 by the International Bible Society. Used by permission of Zondervan Publishing House. The "NIV" and "New International Version" trademarks are registered in the United States Patent and Trademark Office by International Bible Society.

Scripture references marked KJV are taken from the King James Version of the Bible.

Scripture references marked NASB are taken from the New American Standard Bible, © 1960, 1963, 1968, 1971, 1972, 1973, 1975, 1977 by The Lockman Foundation. Used by permission.

ISBN 1-4141-0140-6
Library of Congress Catalog Card Number: 2004101517

This book is dedicated to the members of the Aroma of Christ Prayer Group who have faithfully prayed for the needs of the chemically sensitive throughout the years. It is also dedicated to the millions of others who struggle with Multiple Chemical Sensitivity. May those with MCS know how special they are to God, and that He will always be with them to provide comfort in the storms of life.

Remember your word to your servant, for you have given me hope. My comfort in my suffering is this: Your promise preserves my life. The arrogant mock me without restraint, but I do not turn from your law. I remember your ancient laws, O Lord, and I find comfort in them.

(Psalm 119: 49–52)

For the Lord comforts his people and will have compassion on his afflicted ones.

(Isaiah 49:13)

Table of Contents

Foreword

By David Buscher, M.D.

Multiple Chemical Sensitivity (MCS) is somewhat of a recent medical phenomenon, which is poorly understood, controversial, and difficult to treat. One of the best definitions of this condition was published in the Archives of Environmental Health in 1999, which defined MCS as (1) a chronic condition, (2) with symptoms that recur reproducibly, (3) in response to low levels of exposure, (4) to multiple unrelated chemicals, (5) causing symptoms in multiple organ systems, which (6) improve or resolve when incitants (chemical irritants) are removed.

More simply stated, MCS is a noteworthy condition in which patients exhibit a very high degree of sensitivity to low levels of chemical substances, which can cause a multitude of different symptoms. One of the earliest studies in 1987 suggested that 2–10% of the U.S. population had chemical sensitivity. Later studies from 1993–1996 estimated the numbers had risen to 15–33%, suggesting an increase of MCS within the population. Clinically, physicians who specialize in Environmental Medicine would agree that the incidence of MCS is rising.

The cause of MCS and its growing incidence correlate with the increasing use of an overwhelming diversity of chemicals to which we are all exposed. Chemical exposures are now part of daily life; we are born with toxic chemicals already circulating in our tissues, and the longer we live the more we accumulate. A few of the places where these chemicals are found include our air, water, food, clothing, furniture, and beds. We spend 95% of our time indoors or in cars where chemical toxins are more concentrated. This is only a brief overview of where these chemical exposures can occur.

Total avoidance of chemical toxins is nearly impossible because of the ubiquitous presence of these chemicals throughout our environment. It has been shown that pesticides used in Texas find their way to remote areas such as the Arctic through a process known as "leapfrogging." The level of awareness surrounding the danger from toxic chemicals is generally much higher than it was thirty years ago. This has resulted in increased availability of less toxic building materials, effective air and water filtration systems, healthier cosmetics and personal care products, as well as less chemically contaminated foods. Each of us has the ability to reduce our level of exposure by making informed and healthy choices concerning where we live, what we eat, and what we drink.

Proper stewardship of the earth God has given us requires reduction of the sources of toxic chemicals as much as possible. Perhaps this can be best achieved by grassroots dissemination of information about the chemical problem to our neighbors, schoolteachers, fellow church members, and overworked politicians.

Awareness of the impact of chemical exposures on human health is the first step in bringing about the changes that the people of our nation will implement when properly informed.

David Buscher, M.D., FPAAEM
Former President American Academy of Environmental Medicine
June 2004

Educational background and experience:

David Buscher, M.D. has been specializing in the field of Environmental Medicine for more than 25 years. He is board-certified by the American Board of Environmental Medicine and is past president of the American Academy of Environmental Medicine. He received his medical degree from the State University of New York at Buffalo. After several years of practicing medicine, Dr. Buscher developed an interest in nutritional and environmental influences on disease. He then completed a one and a half-year fellowship at the Human Ecology Research Center under Theron Randolph, M.D., the "Father of Environmental Medicine." Following his mentorship under Dr. Randolph, he completed two years of residency training in Occupational Medicine at the University of Washington. He eventually started his own practice, The Northwest Center for Environmental Medicine, which is located in Bellevue, Washington. You may visit his Web site at: *www.drbuscher.com.*

Preface

$\mathcal{I}$magine taking a walk around the block to get some fresh air and exercise, only to end up having a seizure from exposure to fabric softener fumes drifting out of a neighbor's dryer vent. Or going to a massage therapist and having extremely blurred vision for several hours afterward as a result of being exposed to the toxic oils used. Try to envision what it would be like to go to church anticipating worship, hearing God's Word, and fellowshipping with other believers. Upon arrival at church, a few whiffs of someone's perfume cause severe disorientation, debilitating fatigue, and a migraine, which force you to return home without attending the service. These are just a few of the experiences I have had in my journey with Multiple Chemical Sensitivity.

People who suffer from MCS become ill when exposed to low levels of chemicals that wouldn't bother the average person. When exposed to products such as fresh paint, new carpeting, perfume, and scented laundry detergent, a few of the symptoms people may experience include migraines, seizures, disorientation, joint pain, and asthma attacks. Because reactions to chemical substances vary from person to person, MCS can be a difficult illness for others to understand. For example, five people with MCS exposed to the same chemical may have a variety of reactions, and some may not even react to it at all. This makes it a confusing condition to try to explain to those who don't have it.

One of the biggest needs for people with Multiple Chemical Sensitivity is validation. This is because there is still a lot of ignorance concerning MCS in the medical community and in society at large. It is not uncommon for people who are chemically sensitive to visit ten or more doctors before receiving an accurate diagnosis. People with MCS not only live with physical challenges, but they face significant emotional difficulties as well. Family, friends, neighbors, doctors, and church members often treat them like hypochondriacs because of unfamiliarity with their condition. Many times this leaves a person who is chemically sensitive feeling isolated and rejected at a time when support is needed most. A whole book could be written on the social, economic, and political reasons why MCS is not more widely known. Following are some reasons why recognition has been difficult to achieve.

First of all, using chemicals in everyday life is a fairly recent development in human history. Rosalind Anderson, Ph.D., of Anderson Laboratories, conservatively estimates that over 500,000 chemicals have been introduced into our environment since WWII (*Share, Care and Prayer*, Vol. 21, No. 1, Sept. 2003–March 2004, p.17). Rae Stephenson, a friend of mine whose wife has MCS, made this profound statement: "Those of us who have grown up in the post WWII era are like guinea pigs in an uncontrolled scientific experiment." Since many of the chemicals that are now widely used throughout the world have not been tested for safety to human health, we are beginning to see some of the unfortunate consequences of exposure to these chemicals. The incidence of autoimmune disorders and other chronic illnesses is dramatically increasing—asthma, allergies, fibromyalgia, various types of cancer, Parkinson's, and Alzheimer's are all becoming more prevalent. Researchers are beginning to see that, in some cases, chemical exposures can either be linked to or exacerbate these conditions. (For further study, see "Researching Effects of Chemicals and Pesticides Upon Health" at: *www.chem-tox.com* and "The Environmental Health Network" at: *www.ehnca.org*)

In this country, we often rely on government agencies to protect us in various ways, but the sad fact is that not nearly enough is being done to help guard the health of our nation from toxic chemical exposures. One example of this appears in the book *An Air That Kills* by Andrew Schneider. Andrew uncovered the truth that asbestos in a mine owned by W.R. Grace & Co. was poisoning people in Libby, Montana. In an article in the *Seattle Post-Intelligencer,* August 18, 2000, Andrew tells about his discovery that government agencies such as the E.P.A. had covered up the fact that the mine was very hazardous to those who worked there, as well as to their families and those living in the surrounding area. In the same article, Andrew points out that hundreds of people in Libby have died from asbestosis and other fatal lung diseases brought on by exposure to asbestos. Additionally, it was found that W.R. Grace, lobbyists, politicians, and doctors were involved in the cover-up. (Robert Michael Pyle, "Asbestos Exposé Rips Apart a Deadly Cover-up," *The Seattle Post-Intelligencer,* February 7, 2004.)

I'm afraid that the W.R. Grace story is just the tip of the iceberg when it comes to the covering up of toxic chemical exposures in the workplace. I have read many similar stories occurring in other industries, and I'm sure in years to come we will read of a lot more. Recently, there has been increased awareness about the danger of asbestos, lead, toxic molds, and pesticides. There are plenty of other toxic chemicals, however, that the average consumer still knows nothing about. For example, a lot of people are unaware that in many instances perfume, household cleaners, air fresheners, and other commonly used products contain toxic chemicals. Many people don't find out the truth until they become ill, and by that time, there has often been some long-term damage to their health.

Dan Allen, who was a coach at Holy Cross, announced in 2003 that he suffered from Multiple Chemical Sensitivity. He said that being exposed to chemicals in the environment affected his neuro-muscular system. After being confined to a wheelchair, Allen continued coaching for a while, but after his health declined, he passed away on May 16, 2004. His family is now suing two contractors for allegedly using hazardous substances while refinishing a gymnasium floor in a field house where Allen's office was located. The lawsuit alleges that that the contractors failed to protect people who used the field house from the harmful chemicals they feel were responsible for Allen's illness and death. ("Contractors sued over H.C. coaches death," July 9, 2004, http://sportsillustrated.cnn.com/2004/football/ncaa/07/09/bc.fbc.coach.sdeath.law.ap)

Many corporations need to start facing the truth about the toxicity of their workplaces and/or products they produce. They need to provide safer work environments for their employees, as well as work on formulating non-toxic alternatives for their products. Companies need to put a higher priority on human health than on profits. Prior to her death from pesticide poisoning, Cindy Duehring, recipient of the international Right Livelihood Award in 1997, said the following: "Short-term profits can short-change our future . . . The cost of ignoring the chemical effects on human health is quietly and steadily growing even higher, creating a dangerous risk to the very underpinnings of society." (The Right Livelihood Award, http://www.rightlivelihood.se/recip/duehring.htm)

Another reason there is not more common knowledge about MCS is because our society has become far too dependent on the media for sharing truth with the American public. Sometimes the media is helpful in educating consumers on important facts they need to know about safety issues and other times they are not.

How can society be more supportive of the needs of those with MCS? Since one of the biggest needs for people with MCS is to have their condition legitimatized, those around them should take steps whenever possible to accommodate their special needs. This occurred recently at Calvary Chapel Eastside in Bellevue, Washington. In February of 2004, the pastor and elders decided to welcome *Aroma of Christ,* a ministry to the chemically sensitive, to be part of their church. Calvary Eastside set aside a special room next to the main auditorium they refer to as a "Fragrance Free Zone." On Sunday mornings, people who are chemically sensitive sit in this room where they are able to view the service on a T.V. monitor. Having the special room available helps to insulate them from the people in the congregation who wear fragrances that could make them ill.

As the director of the *Aroma of Christ Ministry,* I lead a nationwide Internet prayer group for those with MCS who are unable to get out and attend church services. There are many Christians around the country who are unable to take part in a traditional church setting due to their chemical sensitivities. Group members can participate in a prayer ministry right from their homes. This helps them feel useful to the body of Christ in the midst of their isolation. The Aroma of Christ Prayer Group provides a place where people with MCS can have their special needs prayed for.

Over the past four years, I have been writing devotionals geared toward people who are chemically sensitive because their situation is so unique. This book is a compilation of those devotionals, which I hope will be one more step in affirming and validating those with MCS. Since I know in my heart that the only way I can make it through this illness is through Christ's help, I want to pass the comfort I have found in Him on to others. My prayer is that people with MCS will find hope and healing for their hurting hearts in these pages. Isaiah 61:1 says:

> *The Spirit of the Sovereign Lord is on me, because the Lord has anointed me to preach good news to the poor. He has sent me to bind up the brokenhearted, to proclaim freedom for the captives and release prisoners from the darkness.*

I hope those of you reading this book who don't have MCS will be able to apply the principles found here to your own trials or struggles.

As you read these pages, may your heart and life be filled with the peace that only He can give.

Acknowledgments

$\mathcal{I}$ have been privileged throughout my life to be influenced by many great men and women of God who have taught me a lot about what it means to be a servant of Jesus Christ; they have helped shape who I am and what I believe. It is my joy to thank a few of the people who have impacted my life greatly.

First, I would like to thank my grandfather, Henry Ness, who left a great spiritual legacy for our family; he was a tremendous example as he poured his life into things that count for eternity. A few years after committing his life to Jesus Christ, Henry left a thriving career at the Standard Oil Company to go into full-time ministry. He pastored several churches throughout his lifetime; in addition, he helped establish numerous branch churches. From 1933–1948, he served as pastor of Calvary Temple in Seattle, Washington. He was also the founder and president of Northwest Bible College in Kirkland, Washington.

Next I'd like to thank my father and mother, Paul and Myrtis Petersen, who taught me that the fear of the Lord is the beginning of wisdom, and that the Bible holds the answers to living a successful life.

I would also like to thank my husband, Dean, who served as a sounding board during the writing of this book. I couldn't have completed this project without his valuable input!

Additionally, I would like to express my heartfelt appreciation to the following people:

My professors at Northwest Bible College, who taught me so much about God's Word.

The various pastors I've gleaned from:

Pastor Charles Anderson—Calvary Temple
Pastor Marty Anderson—Calvary Chapel Bothell
Pastor Robert Case—Calvary Chapel Eastside

Pastor Wayne Taylor for hosting the annual Northwest Pastors' Conferences where I have been inspired through the years by anointed speakers such as Chuck Smith, Jon Courson, Gayle Erwin, Hank Hanegraaff, and many others.

Molly Jensen—a counselor, mentor, and friend who has provided invaluable support during many of the deepest valleys in living with MCS.

Concerning the practical aspects of writing and publishing a book, I'd like to thank my editor, Linda Nathan, of Logos Word Designs, Inc. for her awesome work! In addition, I am grateful for all the input and advice from Roy Gardner, Connie Pitts, Judy Gann, and George and Christina Sollenberger. I'd also like to express my gratitude toward Mr. Ed Walsh, my ninth grade English teacher, for teaching me the basic principles of writing.

Last, and most important, I would like to thank my Lord and Savior, Jesus Christ, who is the greatest role model and teacher of all. To Him be all the glory, honor, and praise!

Introduction

MY MCS JOURNEY

*I*n 1992, I was on top of the world and feeling like I had achieved the all-American dream. I had married Dean, a loving, Christian husband whom I enjoyed sharing life with. In addition, we had purchased our first home on Mercer Island, Washington, and the Lord had provided us with two healthy children. What more could a person ask for? I felt fulfilled in life and thankful for all my blessings. It wasn't long, however, before my perfect world started crumbling around me.

About a year after I gave birth to my son, Brian, I started noticing my body wasn't bouncing back like it had after my first pregnancy. I experienced a lot of fatigue, and my immune system seemed to be weak; I got colds and flu viruses often. One Sunday morning I woke up with red and white patches in the back of my mouth. My husband took me to the emergency room at a local hospital because my regular doctor's office was closed for the weekend.

The following week, my physician got the emergency room doctor's report. He called me, quite concerned, as the initial hospital tests found that I had yeast in my throat, a common symptom of leukemia and AIDS patients. My physician ran tests on me for these two illnesses, and fortunately the results for both were negative.

As time went on, my fatigue worsened, and I was no longer physically able to keep up with the demands of caring for my two children, so I had to put my daughter in daycare several days a week. In addition to the fatigue, I developed unexplained ear pain that lasted for several months. This led me to see an ear, nose, and throat specialist who was unable to find any cause for the pain. In addition, I started experiencing unexplained anxiety attacks that didn't appear to be brought on by stress. Over the next several months, I visited numerous other specialists including an allergist, an internist, an infectious disease specialist, and a naturopath, none of whom could shed any light as to why I was so ill.

Unable to find help from doctors and desperate for answers, I researched the topic of fatigue at the University Bookstore. After reading up on a variety of treatments, I started experimenting with various herbs and supplements. In addition, friends tried to help by introducing me to several different multi-level companies that claimed their products could cure just about anything. After spending thousands of dollars on various remedies sold by these companies, I still found no relief for my fatigue and other symptoms.

At this point, I felt forsaken by God and began to question if He loved me. I identified with Job, who in the midst of his misery said this:

> *Even today my complaint is bitter; his hand is heavy in spite of my groaning. If only I knew where to find him; if only I could go to his*

dwelling! I would state my case before him and fill my mouth with arguments.

(Job 23:2–4)

I was tempted to give up on my faith, but God in his mercy, encouraged me right when I needed it. One Sunday at church, my pastor, Wayne Taylor "just happened" to be talking in his sermon about people who had once served the Lord, yet at some point decided to walk away from their faith. I saw that sermon as a warning from God not to fall into that trap and realized I needed to press on in serving the Lord, even though I had no idea what the future held for me. I love the comforting slogan I saw on a T-shirt during that time that said: "I may not know what the future holds, but I know who holds the future."

My health continued to decline until I was so ill I was forced to be bedridden for several months; I was so sick I couldn't leave my home for any reason, even to walk to the mailbox. I needed help with my kids around the clock, so my mother came over each day to help care for them, as well as to help out with the housework. I wondered if I might be dying, as I had no diagnosis for the illness that was progressively getting worse, and there seemed to be no hope in sight for recovery. I could relate to the psalmist who said: *"My life is consumed by anguish and my years by groaning; my strength fails because of my affliction"* (Psalm 31:10).

In 1994, I finally started to get some help for my health problems when the Lord led me to Dr. Monte Kline, a Clinical Nutritionist in Bellevue, Washington. He found that I had numerous food allergies and Candida, which he treated with homeopathies and various supplements. Being on Dr. Kline's program helped me get my life back. My energy slowly returned, and for a few years, I was able to function fairly normally again. During those years, I mistakenly thought my health problems were over—little did I know there would be many more battles ahead!

Over the next several years, I started noticing that when I was exposed to certain products like pesticides, fresh paint, perfume, and cleaning chemicals, I experienced symptoms such as migraines, disorientation, anxiety, and fatigue. In 1996, I discovered that this condition had a name—Multiple Chemical Sensitivity (MCS). I joined a support group for people with MCS, and I'll never forget the day a group of us met at a local park—what a crazy experience that was! Since we all had reactions to different substances, we couldn't seem to find anywhere to sit and talk that was "safe" for all of us, so we spent most of our time just wandering around the park looking for some air we could all tolerate without becoming ill. Some of the people wore masks, and I remember one man had lined his car with foil to make it "safe" for him. I remember thinking this group was a bit odd, and I sure didn't want to be one of "them!" It was a relief, however, to know I was not the only one on the planet with this unusual illness.

As time went on, I seemed to react quicker and more severely to chemical exposures. I had to avoid certain places such as dry cleaners, moldy buildings, and hardware stores. In 1998, my health really crashed after being exposed to several large doses of toxic fumes on an airplane. Following that incident, I experienced seizures, brain fog, and debilitating fatigue. My sensitivities became so severe that it was almost impossible to leave my home without becoming ill from the various chemical exposures I encountered wherever I went. For example, a simple trip to the grocery store could trigger a seizure from exposure to the fumes from the cleaning products aisle, or when I visited my doctor, I often would become disoriented from exposure to exhaust fumes in the parking lot. I became housebound and bedridden much of the time for a couple of years.

One of the most difficult experiences during those years was missing special events. I was unable to attend my children's performances in school concerts, and I had to miss many weddings and funerals of special friends and family members. One of the few places I could go during those years without becoming ill was a spot up in the mountains near Granite Falls that my husband and I discovered. It was about a forty-five minute drive from our home, and once we got there, we would take about a ten-minute walk in the woods since that was all I had the energy for. There was a beautiful waterfall there, and I immensely enjoyed the opportunity to be out in the midst of God's creation.

My journey in living with Multiple Chemical Sensitivity has taken me through many trials and storms, yet the Lord has been a refuge for me during those times. Isaiah 25:4 says, *"You have been a refuge for the poor, a refuge for the needy in his distress, a shelter from the storm."* I have learned that walking by faith in God is the key to successfully navigating through the twists and turns of living with MCS. A verse my brother, Paul shared at my wedding in 1987 has taken on a deeper meaning to me than ever before. Galatians 2:20 says:

> *I have been crucified with Christ, and I no longer live, but Christ lives in me. The life I live in the body, I live by faith in the Son of God, who loved me and gave himself for me.*

Since 1998, it has been a long, slow journey to regain a certain level of health. Through the help of Dr. David Buscher, Dr. Monte Kline, and Dr. Mitchell Marder, my health has improved significantly over the last six years. I am still chemically sensitive, but not to the severe degree I was following the chemical injury I had on the airplane. I have regained a fair amount of energy and am so thankful to God that I am able to take care of my family again; serving them is the greatest joy and privilege of my life! Even though my lifestyle is still quite limited, I am able to visit quite a few public places again without becoming ill, so for that I am very grateful. I share the sentiment of the psalmist who said:

> *We will tell the next generation the praiseworthy deeds of the Lord,*
> *his power, and the wonders he has done.*
>
> (Psalm 78:4)

Life is always uncertain when living with a chronic illness, but I look forward to the future, knowing that no matter what lies ahead, the Lord will be with me. In Proverbs 31, it says: *"Strength and dignity are her clothing, and she smiles at the future"* (Proverbs 31:25 NASB).

The Scent Queen

Then will I go to the altar of God, to God, my joy and my delight.
(Psalm 43:4)

Prior to having MCS, I was "The Scent Queen." I loved scents! You name it; I loved it. Perfume was one of my favorite fragranced products. Each year on my birthday, my parents would give me money as a gift, and with it, I would typically go to a local department store and purchase a set of scented products, consisting of a perfume and body lotion combination. Potpourri was another fragranced product I enjoyed. My husband used to complain about the abundance of potpourri in our home, as I had a different scent in every room, as well as different varieties for every season. One of my favorite scents was rose, and at Christmas time, I loved the pine-scented potpourri.

A pastime that used to bring me great pleasure was shopping at body and bath shops. I remember one weekend my husband and I took a trip to Whistler, B.C in Canada. I'll never forget the body and bath shop there. I spent an hour or two just going around sniffing all the wonderful scented products—the strawberry bath oil, the watermelon lip-gloss, and the cantaloupe lotion. I thought I was in heaven! I was so overwhelmed with the variety of scented products that I couldn't decide which ones to buy. The sales lady finally pushed me to make a decision. I went home with a carefully selected scented lip-gloss and lotion.

After realizing I had MCS, I was forced to give up my love for scented products. It was a very difficult weaning process for me, to get rid of all the products that had once brought me so much pleasure. The perfume was the first to go. At the time, one of my favorite perfumes was called "Poison." Now I realize what an appropriate name that was for the product! One by one, I gradually had to get rid of my potpourri, lotions, and other scented products. The last thing to go was my scented bath oil, and I remember thinking: *Not my bath oil, too!* But the Lord showed me I had to dispose of it for the sake of my health.

The loss of all these products I once enjoyed forced me to re-examine my life. I had to look at where I was seeking to find joy and fulfillment. Finding pleasure in scented products was not wrong in and of itself, but the Lord showed me that a better place to look for joy was in my relationship with Him. When there are fewer distractions in our lives, it seems easier to put our main focus where it should be—on Him. I now spend more time listening to praise CDs and videotapes, which inspire me to spend time worshipping the Lord privately in my home. I cherish these precious times with the Lord, knowing Jesus is to be my true source of joy in life. Nehemiah 8:10 says: *"The joy of the Lord is your strength."*

David was a great example of someone who found great joy in worshiping and celebrating the Lord with all his might. 2 Samuel

6:5 says: *"David and the whole house of Israel were celebrating with all their might before the Lord, with songs and with harps, lyres, tambourines, sistrums and cymbals."* This week let's enjoy the Lord and find joy in our relationship with Him.

God's Plan in Tragedy

And we know that in all things God works for the good of those who love him, who have been called according to his purpose.

(Romans 8:28)

On January 31, 2000, Alaska Airlines Flight #261 crashed off the coast of southern California, killing all of its passengers. Two of those passengers were Joe and Linda Knight. Prior to the crash, Joe had been the pastor of The Rock Church in Monroe, Washington. He and his wife Linda, were returning from mission work in Puerto Vallarta, Mexico when they lost their lives. To our human eyes, this was indeed a horrible tragedy. However, in the aftermath of the crash, God did some incredible things. Jeff Knight, who is Joe and Linda's son, took over as senior pastor of the church. He and his wife Melinda, are now carrying on the ministry at The Rock Church. I know Joe and Linda would be so proud of them! In the last four years since the crash, the church has tripled in size. To accommodate the growing congregation, The Rock Church built a new facility, which was completed in the spring of 2004.

A few months after the airplane crashed, a local television station did a story about Mission to Mexico, a mission outreach Joe and Linda started. At the end of the news story, they gave information on how people could contribute to the mission. What a wonderful thing for a secular television station to present the need for a mission project! Even though Satan meant the crash for evil, God allowed some good to come out of it. Genesis 50:20 says:

You intended to harm me, but God intended it for good to accomplish what is now being done, the saving of many lives.

Jeff Knight and his sister, Jennifer, along with The Rock Church are determined to carry on Mission to Mexico. The mission project ministers to children who live in a garbage dump by supplying food and clothing, along with medical and dental supplies. Construction of a facility to be used as a community center for the children is near completion. Since Joe and Linda went to be with the Lord, it's exciting to see God expanding the ministries they once led.[1]

God will also bring good out of our struggles in living with MCS if we ask Him to. I have seen God do many good things in my own life as a result of having to deal with chronic illness. For one thing, I am much closer to God and a lot more heavenly minded than I probably ever would've been, had I remained healthy. I now have much more time to pray and meditate on God's Word. Even though our society values accomplishments, God is more concerned about the state of our hearts and our relationship with Him. 2 Chronicles 16:9 says: *"For the eyes of the Lord range throughout the earth to strengthen those whose hearts are fully committed to him."*

This week, I encourage you to ask God to bring some good out of the trials you endure living with MCS. In addition, ask God to purify your heart and make you like Him, accomplishing His plan for your life in the midst of the challenges. God is indeed an expert at working all things in our lives for good if we let Him.

Perseverance

As servants of God we commend ourselves in every way: in great endurance; in troubles, hardships and distresses; in beatings, imprisonments and riots; in hard work, sleepless nights and hunger.
(2 Corinthians 6:4)

Linda Knight was a real inspiration to me. Back in the late nineties, she and her husband Joe often appeared as hosts on a Christian television network. One night as she was sharing about her life, she really encouraged me. That particular night, she said that, while learning to ride horses, her trainer would tell her that when she fell off she needed to get back on the horse. Over and over again her trainer kept encouraging her: "Get back on the horse; get back on the horse."

This simple principle can relate to us in our journeys with MCS as well. So many times after a chemical exposure, I feel beaten down. I often feel like one of those plastic punching bags that my kids had when they were young—you know, the kind where you punch them and they pop back up at you? When I feel that way, the reality is that I must get back up again and keep going. Psalm 71:20 says: *"Though you have made me see troubles, many and bitter, you will restore my life again; from the depths of the earth you will again bring me up."*

Those of us with MCS often feel knocked down by chemical exposures. Perhaps during some of those times you may have felt like Job, who cried out: *"My days are swifter than a weaver's shuttle, and they come to an end without hope. Remember, O God, that my life is but a breath; my eyes will never see happiness again"* (Job 7:6–7). Sometimes after an exposure we may feel so discouraged we just want to give up and quit. The important thing is that we don't let the exposures keep us down for long. We must keep "getting back on the horse." For us, this translates into dusting ourselves off and continuing on in this journey called life. I think those of us with MCS must become masters of perseverance if we are to thrive in the midst of our illness. James 5:11 has this encouragement for us:

> *As you know, we consider blessed those who have persevered. You have heard of Job's perseverance and have seen what the Lord finally brought about. The Lord is full of compassion and mercy.*

Sometimes exposures may lay us up for several days, months, or even years. The important thing is that we continue to have hope. Even if we are so fatigued we are in bed most of the time, it doesn't mean life is over. No matter what the state of our health, we must continue to persevere. Jeremiah 29:11 says:

> *"For I know the plans I have for you,"* declares the Lord, *"plans to prosper you and not to harm you, plans to give you hope and a future."*

Whatever you may be going through today, hang in there, persevere, and when you are able, "get back on the horse."

God's Sovereignty

I am God, and there is no other; I am God, and there is none like me. I make known the end from the beginning, from ancient times, what is still to come. I say: My purpose will stand, and I will do all that I please.

(Isaiah 46:9–10)

*H*ow many of us would've chosen MCS as our lot in life if we had been given a choice? Probably no one! The Christian life is a daily dying to our own wishes, plans, and desires for our lives. This is not always easy. These days we hear so much in Christian circles about God's healing power that we may mistakenly assume that physical healing is our right as children of God. Some of us may wonder, "Why not me, God? If you heal so many others, why won't you heal me?"

An acquaintance of mine, Jim Dolhanyk helped me grapple with that question in my own life. In his early thirties, Jim was diagnosed with melanoma, a very aggressive type of skin cancer.

He had surgery to remove the cancer initially, but, a year later, it was back with a vengeance. The doctors gave him four months to live. During that four-month period, when interviewed by Hank Hanegraaff on the radio program the *Bible Answer Man*, Hank asked Jim, "Would you be healed if you just had enough faith?" I'll never forget Jim's response. He replied, "The question is not, 'Do I have enough faith to be healed?' the question is, 'Do I trust God's sovereignty?'"[2]

Wow! That statement revolutionized my thinking on the whole topic of healing. For the first time in my life, I realized God is not obligated to heal me if I simply have enough faith. On the contrary, God calls me to humble myself and be obedient to whatever plan He has for my life. Sometimes His plan is to heal, but other times it is not. I need to rest in His sovereign plan for my life, even when it may be different from mine. Proverbs 16:9 says: *"In his heart a man plans his course, but the Lord determines his steps."*

Humility and obedience go hand in hand. If we humble ourselves before God, we will willingly accept whatever He allows, even living with a chronic illness like MCS. Isaiah 66:2 says: *"This is the one I esteem: he who is humble and contrite in spirit, and trembles at my word."* Christ humbled himself and was obedient to the point of death. When I think my trial of living with MCS is so great, I need to stop and ponder the humility and obedience of Jesus:

> *Your attitude should be the same as that of Christ Jesus: Who, being in very nature God, did not consider equality with God something to be grasped, but made himself nothing, taking the very nature of a servant, being made in human likeness. And being found in appearance as a man, he humbled himself and became obedient to death— even death on a cross!*
>
> (Philippians 2:5–8)

I'm sure my suffering with MCS will never compare to the depth of Christ's suffering. Today let's meditate on His humility, asking God to work that same quality in our hearts and lives.

Hope

And we rejoice in the hope of the glory of God. Not only so, but we also rejoice in our sufferings, because we know that suffering produces perseverance; perseverance, character; and character, hope.
(Romans 5:2–4)

*H*ave you ever stopped to think that the trial of living with MCS can actually help produce hope in a person's life? Who would ever guess that something as challenging as MCS could actually contribute to having hope? Well, according to Romans 5, this is a distinct possibility! If we view our suffering from God's perspective, it will ultimately produce hope. First our suffering produces perseverance, which in turn produces character. Once godly character is developed in our lives, the natural outcome will be hope.

For those of us who know Christ, we have many reasons to have hope in our lives. One of these is knowing we have the gift of eternal life. Titus 3:7 says: *"So that, having been justified by his grace, we might become heirs having the hope of eternal life."* Another verse that should get us excited about our eternal destiny is Colossians 1:27: *"To them God has chosen to make known among the Gentiles the glorious riches of this mystery, which is Christ in you, the hope of glory."* The *American College Dictionary* defines glory as: "state of splendor, magnificence and greatest prosperity."[3] Now that sounds like something worth looking forward to. Heaven, here we come!

There are so many wonderful Scriptures that talk about the hope we have in our lives because of Christ. I Thessalonians 1:3 says: *"We continually remember before our God and Father your work produced by faith, your labor prompted by love, and your endurance inspired by hope in our Lord Jesus Christ."* According to this verse, our hope in Christ can help us endure the things of this life.

Romans 12:12 has this exhortation for us: *"Be joyful in hope, patient in affliction, faithful in prayer."* Hope often precedes joy. If we have hope, then joy will arise in us as we anticipate good things ahead in the future.

The enemy would like nothing more than for us to lose our hope. Each day we need to guard our minds against thoughts of discouragement that will steal our hope. We need to continue to have hope for our remaining days on this earth. We need to continue to be hopeful that someday there will be a cure for MCS, and hopeful that someday society will understand our plight. We also need to remain hopeful that someday we will be able to venture out and go more places as society becomes more educated on the dangers of chemicals. Another thing to remain hopeful about is that God may choose to partially or fully heal us from MCS at some point in the future.

Today, let us pray that we would allow God to use our suffering with MCS to produce hope in our lives for this life and in the life to come. Never lose your hope!

Suffering

I have been in danger from rivers, in danger from bandits, in danger from my own countrymen, in danger from Gentiles; in danger in the city, in danger in the country, in danger at sea; and in danger from false brothers.

(2 Corinthians 11:26)

*L*ife is difficult. This statement is simple, yet profound. We live in a society that seems to have lost the perspective of the value of suffering. We all seem to want quick fixes for our pain, and would prefer that our lives be smooth sailing. Unfortunately, these types of desires are usually not based on reality.

The summary of the apostle Paul's challenges shows that he certainly didn't have easy circumstances to contend with. His life exemplifies the reality that life is indeed difficult. Living with MCS, we face unique obstacles. Our list of challenges might look something like this: "Twenty times I have been beaten down by pesticides; thirty times I've gone into a toxic rage from being exposed to perfume; I've been in danger from laundry detergents, auto exhaust, and fresh paint. I've experienced migraines because of air fresheners and brain fog from cigarette smoke; I've experienced anxiety attacks from exposure to carpet fumes and endured muscle pain from exposure to dry cleaning chemicals."

Is there anything positive to be gained from enduring pain and suffering while on this planet? Peter shares some incredible wisdom as he tells us about the value of going through trials:

> *In this you greatly rejoice, though now for a little while you may have had to suffer grief in all kinds of trials. These have come so that your faith—of greater worth than gold, which perishes even though refined by fire—may be proved genuine and may result in praise, glory, and honor when Jesus Christ is revealed.*
> (I Peter 1:6–7)

These verses assure us that there is a purpose for our pain, and it is not all for nothing. I recently heard that in a study done on holocaust survivors, one of the common elements present in the lives of the survivors was the belief that there was a purpose for their suffering. The *Wycliffe Bible Commentary* points out that during trials, it is the end result, not the process that should be the focus. It talks about how the results of our tests will far exceed "the gleam of fire-refined gold," which perishes by nature.[4] When our faith is proved genuine, it will result in praise, glory, and honor at the appearing of Jesus Christ.

As we endure various trials in living with MCS, let's take the apostle Paul's advice who said in 2 Timothy 4:5: *"keep your head in all situations, endure hardship,"* knowing that our suffering and the testing of our faith will have eternal significance.

Fulfillment in Life

If anyone else thinks he has reasons to put confidence in the flesh, I have more: circumcised on the eighth day, of the people of Israel, of the tribe of Benjamin, a Hebrew of Hebrews; in regard to the law, a Pharisee; as for zeal, persecuting the church; as for legalistic righteousness, faultless.

(Philippians 3:4–6)

At one point in his life, the apostle Paul took pride in his earthly status and accomplishments. Prior to becoming ill, those of us with MCS may have had similar lists of achievements, including such things as our educational status, our careers, or the ministries we were involved with. MCS stripped many of us of these types of accomplishments that at one time gave us a sense of purpose and fulfillment in our lives. This may have created a vacuum in some people's lives due to the losses they experienced. If this is the case, how should a person fill this void up?

The apostle Paul had a phenomenal perspective that can help us with this question. In Philippians 3:7–8, he says:

But whatever was to my profit I now consider loss for the sake of Christ. What is more, I consider everything a loss compared to the surpassing greatness of knowing Christ Jesus my Lord, for whose sake I have lost all things. I consider them rubbish that I may gain Christ.

Now that is powerful! The apostle Paul considered his past accomplishments "rubbish" in exchange for the joy and privilege of knowing Christ. He realized that true joy and fulfillment in life is found in a relationship with Him.

Paul gives us a great example to strive after: *"I want to know Christ and the power of his resurrection and the fellowship of sharing in his sufferings, becoming like him in his death, and so, somehow, to attain to the resurrection from the dead"* (Philippians 3:10–11). These verses seem to sum up the cry of Paul's heart. In getting to know Christ, Paul not only wanted to know Him intimately, but he also wanted to experience His resurrection power. In addition, he was willing to share in Christ's sufferings, which involved enduring hardships for Christ's sake.

Today I encourage you to make your relationship with Christ the number one pursuit in your life. Psalm 27:4 says:

One thing I ask of the Lord, this is what I seek: that I may dwell in the house of the Lord all the days of my life, to gaze upon the beauty of the Lord and to seek him in his temple.

In addition to seeking God, avail yourself of Christ's resurrection power: *"His divine power has given us everything we need for life and godliness"* (2 Peter 1:3). Lastly, we should be willing to suffer for His sake. 2 Timothy 2:11–12 says: *"If we died with him, we will also live with him; if we endure, we will also reign with him."*

If we pour our lives into these pursuits, I believe great fulfillment awaits us.

He Will Carry You

May he send you help from the sanctuary and grant you support from Zion.

(Psalm 20:2)

As I was preparing to leave from Seattle to fly to Palm Springs with my daughter in February of 1998, I felt a sense of apprehension about stepping on a plane as an MCS sufferer, knowing there was the potential danger of being exposed to any number of toxic substances. The anxiety was particularly acute because I knew that if I became ill from an exposure there would be no way of escape. In light of this, I called a friend the night before my flight to ask for prayer. Theri prayed for me, and afterward her encouragement to me was: "Remember Janine, no matter what happens on the flight Jesus will carry you."

On February 6, my husband drove my daughter and me to the airport. I made it through the airport without any chemical exposures, and once I boarded the plane the first part of our flight was rather uneventful. As we neared our destination however, my so far perfect flight turned into an MCS sufferer's nightmare. We hit a severe storm, which resulted in three aborted landing attempts. After each failed attempt, the plane shot back up in the air, each time allowing toxic fumes that smelled like jet fuel to enter the cabin through the ventilation system. Inhaling the vapors caused me to become very fatigued, dizzy, and disoriented.

The decision was made to re-route our plane to the Ontario airport, which is an hour and a half drive from Palm Springs. Upon arriving in Ontario, the airlines decided to shuttle all the passengers on a diesel bus to get us to our final destination. Yikes! I couldn't handle the thought of being exposed to any more toxic fumes at this point since I was already very ill. I felt as though I had been drugged and was having a hard time functioning. In the physical state I was in, I wondered how on earth my eight-year old daughter and I were going to get to Palm Springs safely. All of a sudden the words of my friend Theri rang in my mind: "Jesus will carry you." Those words gave me the hope and strength I needed to carry on at one of the most difficult moments of my life.

The words of my friend Theri proved to be true. The next several hours God showed His magnificent power and faithfulness to me as He worked out all the details to get us to Palm Springs in spite of the fact that I felt brain dead. The first provision came in the way of the airlines offering us our own private shuttle van, once I explained I could not tolerate a diesel bus due to my health condition. Another blessing came when a total stranger helped us retrieve a luggage cart from clear across the airport. Once we had the cart, my daughter was a blessing as she pushed it around until we reached our shuttle.

For reasons beyond my human comprehension, God allowed one of my worst nightmares to come true—being trapped on an airplane with dangerous fumes and nowhere to run! On this earth, God does not always spare us from pain and suffering, but He does promise to help us through whatever difficulties we may find ourselves in if we call on Him to help us. Psalm 22:24 says: *"For he has not despised or disdained the suffering of the afflicted one; he has not hidden his face from him but has listened to his cry for help."*

Whatever challenging situation you may find yourself in today, I encourage you to call on the name of Jesus and He will carry you through.

Flowers After the Rain

*See, I have refined you, though not as silver; I have tested you in the
furnace of affliction.*

(Isaiah 48:10)

$\mathcal{B}$ack in the winter of 1998, all four of my parents' children
flew to Palm Springs to visit them on separate occasions. My three
healthy siblings had normal flights going down there. Being the
only daughter who is chemically sensitive, I was the one who ended
up on a flight where I was exposed to large doses of toxic fumes
that resulted in a debilitating chemical injury. Afterward, this did
not make sense to me. I believe God is sovereign and could've
prevented me from getting on that particular flight, so why did He
let this happen? It just didn't seem fair to me. I started asking the
age-old question: "Why does God allow pain and suffering?"

In January 1998, I wrote down thirteen areas of my life that I
prayed the Lord would help me improve in that year. The following December as I was reviewing the list, I realized the Lord had

done some work in every single area I had prayed about! I was amazed that the Lord used my chemical injury in February as a catalyst to prune me in a lot of areas that needed it. After figuring this out, I said, "Thank you God for my chemical injury." I quickly caught myself, realizing what I had just said. If you had asked me in February if I ever would have been able to thank God for the chemical injury I had just experienced, I would've said, "No way! What good could come out of something so traumatic?" Well, I can honestly say today that I am thankful for it; I'm not thankful for the pain, but I am grateful for the tremendous things God has done through it—it really was a gift. Hebrews 2:10 says: *"It was fitting that God, for whom and through whom everything exists, should make the author of their salvation perfect through suffering."*

One of the reasons God allows pain and suffering in our lives is to refine our character, so that we might become the people He created us to be. Prior to my chemical injury, I had exceedingly high expectations of myself. I felt I had to be the perfect wife, the perfect mom, the perfect friend, the perfect daughter, and on and on the list went. I realize now that I was my own worst enemy. The Lord has shown me that His expectations for me are far different than my own. Matthew 11:28–30 says this:

> *Come to me, all you who are weary and burdened, and I will give you rest. Take my yoke upon you and learn from me, for I am gentle and humble in heart, and you will find rest for your souls. For my yoke is easy and my burden is light.*

Prior to my injury, I was running fast, trying to please everyone around me. Since then, I have learned that the only one I need to please in life is my heavenly Father. He has helped me simplify my life and re-order my priorities. In addition, He has helped me focus on what matters most to me in life—my faith, friends, and family.

Today, whatever trial you may be facing, let the Lord use your pain to prune you. Ask Him to help you simplify your life, re-order your priorities, and seek to please Him alone. If you do this, you will see "flowers after the rain."

Not My Home!

For he was looking forward to the city with foundations, whose architect and builder is God.

(Hebrews 11:10)

*D*uring the time I first realized I was chemically sensitive, I walked into a dry cleaners and was overpowered by a thick stench of toxic chemicals. After taking one breath of toxic air, I quickly turned on my heels and headed back to my car. The first thought that came to mind was: *This world is not my home!* From that day forward, I have been very aware of the fact that this earth is a brief, temporary residence as I look forward to a better, permanent home God is preparing for me in heaven. Hebrews 11:16 says: *"Instead, they were longing for a better country—a heavenly one. Therefore God is not ashamed to be called their God, for he has prepared a city for them."* Isn't it exciting to think that God has a heavenly city waiting for those of us who believe in Him when we leave this earth?

Another experience I had that accentuated the fact that this earth is not my home took place at my cousin's wedding. As I entered the church where the wedding was being held, the whole auditorium wreaked like a perfume counter at a department store. The auditorium had three levels of balconies, so I tested each balcony to see if I could find some "safe" air, but to no avail. I couldn't believe that nobody else at the wedding seemed to notice that the entire auditorium stunk! At that point I really felt like an alien from another planet who did not belong on this earth. I did end up sitting in the highest balcony with my mask on through most of the wedding, but I paid for it the next day with extreme fatigue and a migraine brought on by the chemical exposure.

If you have ever felt like an alien or stranger on this earth, rejoice! It's okay to feel that way because that is what the Bible teaches—that we are "aliens and strangers" in this world (I Peter 2:11). We are just passing through as we head toward our eternal destiny, and God wants us to live our lives conscious of that fact. He desires that we look forward with anticipation to the day when we will see Jesus face to face. Prior to Jesus leaving the earth to go back to heaven, He comforted His disciples with these words:

> *Do not let your hearts be troubled. Trust in God; trust also in me. In my Father's house are many rooms; if it were not so, I would have told you. I am going there to prepare a place for you. And if I go and prepare a place for you, I will come back and take you to be with me that you also may be where I am.*
>
> (John 14:1–2)

Today let's try to envision our eternal homes, remembering the fact that Jesus promised to take us there someday:

For the Lord himself will come down from heaven, with a loud command, with the voice of the archangel and with the trumpet call of God, and the dead in Christ shall rise first. After that, we who are still alive and are left will be caught up together with them in the clouds to meet the Lord in the air. And so we will be with the Lord forever.

(I Thessalonians 4:16–17)

Hallelujah! Now that's something worth getting excited about!

Depression

Now, O Lord, take away my life, for it is better for me to die than to live.

(Jonah 4:3)

For years, whenever I faced seasons of depression, it was something I preferred to keep secret. During those times, I felt guilty as a Christian for feeling so low. I didn't want anyone to find out this was a problem for me, because I thought depression was a sign of weakness or a lack of spirituality. As I finally started opening up to friends about this particular battle, I found out I was in good company! I soon discovered that most of my friends had struggled with some form of depression at one time or another as well. In addition, I started realizing that many of the people God greatly used throughout history also faced times of depression. Elijah, Jonah, Jeremiah, and David are just a few examples of Biblical characters who dealt with this problem.

Sometimes the pressures of life become almost unbearable. Jeremiah was a prophet who proclaimed God's judgment against Judah for a period of over forty years.[5] Because of this, he endured a lot of persecution. On one occasion after prophesying in the court of the Lord's temple, Jeremiah was beaten and put in stocks due to an order by a priest named Pashhur.[6] Listen to how desperate Jeremiah felt after this happened:

> *Cursed be the day I was born! May the day my mother bore me not be blessed! Cursed be the man who brought my father the news, who made him very glad, saying, "A child is born to you—a son!"*
> (Jeremiah 20:14–15)

Those of us who suffer from a chronic illness are especially prone to depression for obvious reasons. We often feel physically ill, we have experienced many losses in our lives, and, in addition, our depression can often be physiological in origin. Many of my worst bouts of depression have occurred after an exposure to chemicals such as new paint, auto exhaust, and perfume. Often a chemical depression won't lift until our bodies have had a chance to detoxify them.

There is no simple cure for depression. It is a very complex problem with multiple causes, including physical, emotional, and spiritual. Sometimes prayer or counseling can help, sometimes getting our eyes off ourselves and doing something for others can help, and sometimes, we just need to persevere until it lifts. Psalm 40:1–3 says:

> *I waited patiently for the Lord; he turned to me and heard my cry. He lifted me out of the slimy pit, out of the mud and mire; he set my feet on a rock and gave me a firm place to stand. He put a new song in my mouth, a hymn of praise to our God.*

If you are going through a period of depression right now, ask God to show you the specific cause and what you should do about it. Hang in there and ask God to lift you out of the pit in His timing. Psalm 30:5 has this encouragement for us: *"Weeping may remain for a night, but rejoicing comes in the morning."*

A Faithful Friend

My friends and companions avoid me because of my wounds; my neighbors stay far away.

(Psalm 38:11)

Most of us have experienced the rejection of family or friends due to the challenges MCS presents in relationships. Even though some of my friends have stuck faithfully by my side through the ups and downs of MCS, others have disappeared into thin air. Some people I used to go places and do things with now prefer to hang out with those who are able to be more active and whom they don't have to make special accommodations for. This illness has certainly shown me who my true friends are!

Job was one man who experienced tremendous losses in the area of relationships. Hear what he said about his situation: *"He has alienated my brothers from me; my acquaintances are completely estranged from me. My kinsmen have gone away; my friends have forgotten me. All my intimate friends detest me; those I love have turned against me"* (Job 19:13–14, 19). Perhaps you can relate to Job.

The apostle Paul experienced desertion by his friends at times as well. Here is what happened to him: *"At my first defense, no one came to my support, but everyone deserted me. May it not be held against them. But the Lord stood at my side and gave me strength, so that through me the message might be fully proclaimed and all the Gentiles might hear it"* (2 Timothy 4:16–17).

Though friends and family may reject or desert us at times, the good news is, God will always be there by our sides to give us strength to carry on. Listen to these comforting words by Jesus:

You are my friends if you do what I command. I no longer call you servants, because a servant does not know his master's business. Instead, I have called you friends, for everything that I learned from my Father I have made known to you.

(John 15:14–15)

What an honor to think that Jesus calls those of us who are His followers "friends!" It blesses me greatly to know that the God of the universe considers me to be a friend of His.

Through the years, I've learned to trust the Lord to bring friends into my life that He knows are best for me. Friends on this earth may come and go, but my best friend will always be the Lord. He promises to be with me no matter what. Proverbs 18:24 says: *"A man of many companions may come to ruin, but there is a friend who sticks closer than a brother."*

Today, let's rejoice in the faithful friend we have in Jesus!

The Battle is the Lord's

"But Lord," Gideon asked, "how can I save Israel? My clan is the weakest in Manasseh, and I am the least in my family." The Lord answered, "I will be with you, and you will strike down all the Midianites together."

(Judges 6:15–16)

The battle is much too big! There is no way we can possibly win this battle! This is how I have felt many times when looking at the obstacles we are up against in our struggles with MCS. One battle that has seemed overwhelming to me is the battle for "fragrance free" public places. From a human perspective, it seems impossible that we would ever again be able to mingle in mainstream society without becoming ill from fragrances. Imagine being able to go to a mall, a church, or a theater, knowing that the air would be "fragrance free." Do you think this is an impossible goal?

Gideon faced a battle in his life that seemed insurmountable from human eyes. God commanded Gideon's army of 300 men to fight against the army of the Midianites, which numbered 135,000 men. From a human perspective, this idea seemed ludicrous. In Judges 7:7, God promised this to Gideon: "*The Lord said to Gideon: 'With the three hundred men that lapped I will save you and give the Midianites into your hands.'*" God kept His promise and helped Gideon and the Israelites defeat the army of the Midianites with a mere 300 men!

Another miracle that inspires me is when God delivered the Israelites from slavery under Pharoah in Egypt. Moses told the people: "*Do not be afraid. Stand firm and you will see the deliverance the Lord will bring you today . . . The Lord will fight for you; you need only to be still*" (Exodus 14:13–14). God parted the Red Sea and made a path so the Israelites could escape from Pharoah and his army. After the Israelites passed safely through the dry land, God caused the water to come down upon the Egyptians, and every single one of them drowned. Following this miracle, Moses and the Israelites sang this song to the Lord:

> *Who among the gods is like you, O Lord? Who is like you—majestic in holiness, awesome in glory, working wonders? You stretched out your right hand and the earth swallowed them.*
>   (Exodus 15:11–12)

With the sovereign God of the universe on our side, anything is possible. Halifax, Nova Scotia has become the first major center in North America to prohibit the wearing of all cosmetic fragrances in most indoor places including municipal offices, libraries, hospitals, classrooms, courts, and mass transit busses.[6] Just as God worked on the behalf of those with MCS in this instance, I know He will help us win more battles as well. Psalm 9:12 says: "*He does not ignore the cry of the afflicted.*"

No matter how great the battles facing you may seem, no battle is too big for the God of Abraham, Isaac, and Jacob. The next time you feel overwhelmed with the challenges that lie before you, remember the miracles that God performed time and time again for the Israelites. The same God that helped them is there for you and me.

My Greatest Passion

My soul will be satisfied as with the richest of foods; with singing lips my mouth will praise you.

(Psalm 63:5)

Many of us with MCS have a difficult time dining out without becoming ill from chemical exposures. One of my favorite restaurants that I have found that usually works okay for me is called Mardinis. My favorite menu item is the Chicken Dijon. It is a lightly breaded, moist breast of chicken with a delectable sauce. It is typically served with rice pilaf and fresh sautéed vegetables. It is absolutely mouthwatering, and I leave the restaurant feeling like my appetite has been richly satisfied. This delicious entrée reminds me of Psalm 63, which talks about our soul being satisfied as with the richest of foods when we seek the Lord and praise Him for who He is.

As I think about my goals in life and what I am living for, I want my greatest passion in life to be to seek the Lord and to spend time worshipping Him, allowing Him to mold me into His image. I want the cry of my heart to echo the psalmist David who said in Psalm 63:1: *"O God, you are my God, earnestly I seek you; my soul thirsts for you, my body longs for you, in a dry and weary land where there is no water."* I realize that nothing this world has to offer will provide lasting satisfaction. Only through my relationship with Christ will I ever be truly satisfied.

David Brainerd was someone who modeled the type of passion for Jesus I'd like to have. He was a missionary to the American Indians back in the 1700s. Even though he became an ordained minister in 1742, he decided to give up a life of comfort and ease to ride on horseback and live in the wilderness in order to minister to the Indians in New York, New Jersey, and Pennsylvania. He not only gave up the life of associating with eminent scholars and friends, but he also gave up the opportunity to marry the love of his life, Jerusha, in order to do this.[7] In a letter written to his brother John in 1743, David said this: "There is no happiness and plenary satisfaction to be enjoyed in earthly friends though ever so near and dear, or in any enjoyment that is not God himself."[8] David realized that the greatest satisfaction in life was to be found in Christ, not other people.

Psalm 63:3 says: *"Because your love is better than life, my lips will glorify you."* I think David Brainerd was a person who, like the psalmist, realized that God's love was better than life itself. In a letter to a friend he said, "Never expect any satisfaction or happiness from the world. If you hope for happiness in the world, hope for it from God and not from the world."[9]

David's greatest passion was to serve and love Jesus no matter what the cost. His life was one of total commitment to Jesus Christ. He inspired many to seek a life of sacrifice and holiness as opposed to ease and selfishness. He is quoted in a letter to a friend as saying, "There is no true satisfaction but in God."[10]

Like David Brainerd, let's seek to make Jesus Christ our greatest passion in life and find our satisfaction in Him.

Spiritual Warfare

Now have come the salvation and the power and the kingdom of our God, and the authority of his Christ. For the accuser of our brothers, who accuses them before our God day and night, has been hurled down.

(Revelation 12:10)

o you ever hear thoughts come into your head such as: *Your life is worthless; you really made a fool out of yourself; you are a burden to people?* If so, you are in good company. These are the typical sorts of lies Satan loves to feed all of us. The lies may be different for you, but the enemy knows our weaknesses. He will try to discourage us in the areas of our lives where we are most vulnerable.

Those of us who live with chronic illness have plenty of reasons to feel insecure. It's easy for the enemy to try and torment us, because we have an abundance of limitations and challenges we face every day. John 8:44 says this about Satan:

He was a murderer from the beginning, not holding to the truth, for there is no truth in him. When he lies, he speaks his native language, for he is a liar and the father of lies.

Almost every day, Satan throws his various lies at us. During these times, it is important that we filter those lies through the truths found in God's Word. Isaiah 54:17 says: *"No weapon forged against you will prevail, and you will refute every tongue that accuses you. This is the heritage of the servants of the Lord."*

Sometimes Satan uses comments by other people to attack us. Nehemiah, who was a servant and cupbearer to King Artexerxes I, was a witness to these types of tactics. After hearing that the walls in Jerusalem needed to be rebuilt, Nehemiah got permission from the king to go there and help oversee this project.[11] After the rebuilding had begun, a man by the name of Sanballat started ridiculing the Jews who were working hard along with Nehemiah on this task. He taunted the people by saying:

"What are these feeble Jews doing? Will they restore the wall? Will they offer sacrifices? Will they finish in a day? Can they bring the stones back to life from those heaps of rubble—burned as they are?"
(Nehemiah 4:2)

As if those comments weren't bad enough, listen to what Sanballat's friend, Tobiah, added:

"What they are building—if even a fox climbed up on it, he would break down their wall of stones!"
(Nehemiah 4:3)

No matter how long we've known the Lord, the attacks from Satan never cease. The good news is, we are on the winning team, and we have been given power over Satan through the blood of Jesus. I John 4:4 has this encouragement for us: *"The one who is in you is greater than the one who is in the world."* When the lies and attacks come, we need to reject them in Jesus' name. When Satan tempted Jesus in the wilderness, He responded by saying: "Away from me, Satan!" (Matthew 4:10) We should follow His example when the enemy tempts us as well.

In 2 Timothy 4:18, the apostle Paul says this: *"The Lord will rescue me from every evil attack and will bring me safely to his heavenly kingdom. To him be glory for ever and ever."*

Today, let us praise God for the victory that is promised us through Christ!

God's Promises

Never will I leave you; never will I forsake you.

(Hebrews 13:5)

When I was a child, I took clean air, food, and water for granted. I never dreamed that such a bizarre condition like MCS would someday be a reality for me. I erroneously assumed I would always be able to participate freely in life without concern about where the next "land mine" of chemicals might explode in my face. Sometimes I long to have that type of freedom again.

When I first discovered I had MCS, I was devastated. I knew the problem was way too big for me to handle on my own and that I needed God's strength to make it through. Throughout the years, I have learned to cling to God's promises during the difficult times. Sometimes my faith is strong and at other times it is weak, but I always come back to the reality that my only hope is in God and His Word. Psalm 119:92 says: *"If your law had not been my delight, I would have perished in my affliction."*

Kerry Monroe is a woman who has been an inspiration to many as she has learned to cling to God's promises through some very difficult challenges. First, she watched her husband slowly die of cancer over a six-year period. In addition, a few weeks prior to her husband's death, her son was diagnosed with leukemia. He faced many grueling months of chemotherapy treatments, and on many occasions the prognosis was not good. During those difficult days, Kerry wrote the following prayer: "I draw near and call out to You this day. What I perceive before me is impossible by the way of my own strength and it is essential for me to release it entirely over to You. I will not reminisce of bygone times or of a season yet to come, for my need of Your provision is for this very moment. Prepare and empower me for this day's battle, and in You, God, I can forge further on."

Many intense battles face those of us with MCS. Even in the midst of the worst trials imaginable, the promises found in God's Word will give us the right perspective to help us through. Since we are isolated at home much of the time, sometimes Satan tries to make us think everyone else out there in the world is having a great life while we have a multitude of problems. However, the reality is that everyone has challenges in life. There will always be some people with more severe problems than us, and others who appear to have fewer struggles. As humans, we are all in the same boat as we face the ups and downs of life. Psalm 90:10 talks about the reality of life on this planet:

The length of our days is seventy years—or eighty, if we have the strength; yet their span is but trouble and sorrow, for they quickly pass, and we fly away.

Today you may be struggling with health issues, financial challenges, or relationship problems. Whatever you may be dealing with, cling to God' promises. I love this powerful verse: *"Not one of all the Lord's good promises to the house of Israel failed; every one was fulfilled"* (Joshua 21:45). Remember that God has promised never to leave you or forsake you. He will carry you through the darkest night.

Finding True Joy

Satisfy us in the morning with your unfailing love, that we may sing for joy and be glad all our days.

(Psalm 90:14)

Have you ever been guilty of looking for happiness in outward circumstances? I know I have. As many young girls do, I dreamed about growing up, getting married, and having children, thinking this would bring me ultimate happiness in life. Once I attained these goals, however, I discovered they didn't bring me the satisfaction I was looking for.

King Solomon was a man who searched extensively to find meaning in life. Listen to what his journey entailed:

I wanted to see what was worthwhile for men to do under heaven during the few days of their lives. I amassed silver and gold for myself, and the treasure of kings and provinces. I acquired men and women singers, and a harem as well—the delights of the heart of man. I became greater by far than anyone in Jerusalem before me.

Yet when I surveyed all that my hands had done and what I had toiled to achieve, everything was meaningless, a chasing after the wind; nothing was gained under the sun.

(Ecclesiastes 2:3,8–9,11)

Imagine that after all the earthly wealth Solomon was able to acquire, he said it was meaningless!

Over and over in life, when we achieve or acquire something we thought would bring us happiness, it rarely brings the fulfillment we expected. Why is this? In *A Path Through Suffering*, Elisabeth Elliot says this: "The resurrection, however, is the anchor of our hope. We know that heaven is not *here*, it's *there*. If we were given all we wanted here, our hearts would settle for this world rather than the next."[12] She has hit on something profound here. God doesn't want us to become too attached to this earth, because He knows this world is brief, and the things of this earth don't ultimately satisfy. He wants us to enjoy being in His presence on this earth, and to look forward to heaven where we will be in His presence forever. Psalm 16:11 says: *"You will fill me with joy in your presence, with eternal pleasures at your right hand."*

One advantage of having MCS is that we have been stripped of many of the earthly possessions, pleasures, and activities we once enjoyed. Because of that, I think in some ways it can be easier for us to come to the place where we realize our relationship with God is what brings true meaning to our lives. If we let it, MCS can be a tool to help us find joy in our Creator.

Personally, I have found that the most basic truth in life worth grasping is that true joy in this life and in the life to come is found in being in the presence of the Lord. Psalm 105:3–4 says: *"Glory in his holy name; let the hearts of those who seek the Lord rejoice. Look to the Lord and his strength; seek his face always."*

Today, I encourage you to seek His face and find true joy in His presence!

Coping with Loss

And they admitted that they were aliens and strangers on earth.
(Hebrews 11:13)

Every so often I have days when I wish there were a rocket destined for heaven that I could climb into. Some days I long to be in my heavenly home where there will be no more sickness or pain. This past week I had a few days like that. As my neighbors sprayed generous amounts of herbicides, I found myself feeling very frustrated that it is legal to spray cancer-causing poisons into the air we all breathe. The particular herbicide sprayed has been linked to lymphoma in some people, yet I had no choice but to be exposed to it as it drifted onto my property. For four days in a row, I could detect the pungent stench of herbicides lingering in the air whenever I stepped outside for a moment. On those beautiful sunny days when I would've loved to have been outside in my backyard enjoying God's beautiful creation, I was forced to be stuck inside breathing stale, tainted air.

Accentuating my feeling of confinement was a pile of invitations to events that I would be unable to attend this month due to my illness. Among them were two wedding invitations, along with an invitation to my aunt and uncle's fiftieth wedding anniversary. Sometimes the losses due to MCS seem staggering, and as I was feeling overwhelmed, I opened my Bible to Hebrews 11. As I read it, I was comforted by the fact that saints throughout the ages have endured deep, painful trials, and many were certainly much worse than mine. Look what some of them had to endure:

Some faced jeers and flogging, while still others were chained and put in prison. They were stoned; they were sawed in two; they were put to death by the sword. They went about in sheepskins and goatskins, destitute, persecuted and mistreated—the world was not worthy of them. They wandered in deserts and mountains, and in caves and holes in the ground.

(Hebrews 11:36–38)

Moses was one Biblical character who faced many challenges. Hebrews 11:27 gives us a glimpse into his secret of persevering during difficult times. It says: *"He persevered because he saw him who is invisible."* To make it successfully through the trials of MCS, we need to emulate Moses' example of keeping our eyes on Jesus, not our circumstances. A hymn I sang as a child by Helen H. Lemmel says:

Turn your eyes upon Jesus,
Look full in His wonderful face,
And the things of earth will grow strangely dim,
In the light of His glory and grace.

My former pastor, Rev. Charles Anderson, shared this quote with his congregation years ago: *"Look around you and be distressed.*

Look within you and be depressed. Look at Jesus and your heart will be at rest." Today, let's remember to keep our eyes on Jesus and our hearts will be at rest!

The Greatest Gift

For God so loved the world that he gave his one and only Son, that whoever believes in him shall not perish but have eternal life.

(John 3:16)

Prior to having MCS, Lori Oneal had achieved many of the things the world tells us we need in order to live a happy and successful life. For several years, she worked in the travel industry and had many opportunities to go on various trips and cruises. In addition, for a few years she enjoyed a successful real estate career, winning numerous awards for her outstanding sales. In her spare time, Lori was very active in sports such as skiing, tennis, and softball. In 1991, however, Lori's life drastically changed. During that time, she lived in a moldy apartment with a gas leak. With the toxic exposures in her life, Lori experienced symptoms such as debilitating fatigue, migraines, and sinusitis. Her health deteriorated to the point she feared she might be dying.

Because of her declining health, Lori lost many of the things in life she depended on for security. Feeling there was nowhere to turn in life but up, Lori lifted her face to the heavens, acknowledging that God is the Creator of the universe and the giver of eternal life. Lori committed her life to Jesus Christ and found hope through a relationship with Him. Romans 6:23 says: *"For the wages of sin is death, but the gift of God is eternal life in Christ Jesus our Lord."* Lori readily accepted this free gift.

In the book of John, Jesus claims to be the one and only way to eternal life (John 14:6). In our society today, some people think that there are numerous paths to God. If you believe what the Bible teaches, however, there is only one way to God and eternal life, and that is through a commitment to Jesus Christ. The ultimate questions people need to ask themselves in regard to Jesus, are whether or not they believe He is who He claims to be, and, if so, will they accept His free gift of salvation?

Romans 10:9 says: *"If you confess with your mouth, 'Jesus is Lord,' and believe in your heart that God raised him from the dead, you will be saved."* What this verse refers to is the fact that we need to have a mental belief in Jesus in order to be saved. In addition, when it talks about "believe in your heart," this refers to a commitment of our life to Jesus, similar to that of a marriage commitment between a husband and wife. It is not enough to just believe mentally in God in order to be saved. As it says in James 2:19: *"You believe that there is one God. Good! Even the demons believe that—and shudder."* What is important is that we give up the right to live life our own way and are willing to obey the Word of God no matter what the cost.

As we commit our lives to Jesus, He will change us from the inside out. He will slowly take away our desires for the things that displease Him and will give us new desires that are in line with His will for our lives. As we look to the Lord for strength, He will be there to help us through any trial that should come our way. Like Lori found, the greatest gift that can come about as a result of having MCS is when people realize their need for Christ and ask Him into their lives. Today, if you have not committed your life to Christ, I urge you to accept His free gift of eternal life.

Armed and Dangerous

Your statutes are my delight; they are my counselors.

(Psalm 119:24)

After returning from Palm Springs in 1998, I faced one of the biggest battles of my life as multiple health challenges ensued. Following the chemical injury I incurred on an airplane, day after day I faced debilitating fatigue, seizures, and extreme chemical sensitivity. I became somewhat of a shut-in, as ninety percent of the time I stepped out of my home to go somewhere I became ill. A simple walk around the block caused a seizure if I was exposed to toxic laundry fumes coming out of dryer vents in the neighborhood. A whiff of someone's perfume at church, or auto exhaust in a parking lot, caused extreme disorientation and fatigue that would make it difficult to function.

It was a challenge to get to the doctor during those days, as my husband was busy working and trying to provide for the family. Finding someone "safe" to drive me there was nearly impossible. I reacted to the slightest chemical exposure, including fragrances in the hair products people had used the week before that were still lingering in their hair. I didn't let that stop me though, and I made weekly visits to the doctor anyway in a desperate attempt to get well.

One day while I was in the doctor's office waiting for the nurse to come start a vitamin I.V., I was filled with fear. Even though there were benefits from the I.V.s, they made my symptoms worse right afterward. They often brought on multiple seizures and difficulty breathing while I was detoxing. Apprehensive about what lay ahead, I opened my Bible, and a very comforting verse "just happened" to pop out at me. It was Psalm 41:3, which said: *"The Lord will sustain him on his sickbed and restore him from his bed of illness."* I distinctly felt the Lord impressing upon me that this verse was a promise for my situation. Filled with a glimmer of hope, I went home and posted it everywhere I could think of, on places such as walls, mirrors, and my night stand. I clung to that verse in the months to come when I needed encouragement.

God's Word is one of the most powerful weapons we have available to us when facing adversity. Psalm 119:98–100 says: *"Your commands make me wiser than my enemies, for they are ever with me. I have more insight than all my teachers, for I meditate on your statutes. I have more understanding than the elders, for I obey your precepts."* Imagine that! God's Word is filled with principles that will give us great wisdom and insight beyond our years no matter what challenges lie before us.

Whatever battles you may be facing today, take advantage of the weapon of God's Word. Post verses that pertain to your situation somewhere visible so that the Word of God will saturate your mind and life. It will help give you the strength to carry on when the enemy launches his attacks to try and discourage you. If you cling to God's Word, you will indeed become "armed and dangerous!"

Courage

Have I not commanded you? Be strong and courageous. Do not be terrified; do not be discouraged, for the Lord your God will be with you wherever you go.

(Joshua 1:9)

Years ago, I thought a person with courage was someone who had it all together and never struggled with doubts or fears. I now realize, though, that courage is not the absence of fear. Instead, it is moving ahead in spite of it. I love how Pastor Marty Anderson describes it: "Fear + Action = Courage."

There have been many occasions when I have struggled with fear during my journey with MCS. Numerous times I have experienced symptoms that my doctors had no answers for. During those times, it was easy to get frightened, wondering what was wrong with me and how I was going to get rid of the symptoms. Several times the Lord led me to answers through various means such as friends or books.

When living with a chronic illness, there are a lot of unknowns, which can puzzle us. In light of this, it is important to be filled with courage—courage to move ahead in spite of the uncertainties that go along with MCS. In the Helpfinder section of the *TouchPoint Bible* it says: "Courage is like a chain—we gain or lose courage by watching others, and others gain or lose courage by watching us."[13] As we have courage in the midst of our challenges with MCS, we can be an encouragement to others who may be struggling in their journey. We can let others know that if we can make it through the battles, so can they.

When the Israelite soldiers were in the midst of war, it was recommended they go home if they were frightened, so their fear wouldn't spread to others. Deuteronomy 20:8 says: "*Then the officers shall add, 'Is any man afraid or fainthearted? Let him go home so that his brothers will not become disheartened too.'*" This shows the importance of keeping our attitude positive. Deuteronomy 20: 3–4 says:

> *Hear O Israel, today you are going into battle against your enemies. Do not be fainthearted or afraid; do not be terrified or give way to panic before them. For the Lord your God is the one who goes with you to fight for you against your enemies to give you victory.*

Just as the Israelites needed to have courage in their battles, so we need to continue to have courage in ours as well. Listen to this exhortation: "*For God did not give us a spirit of timidity, but a spirit of power, of love and of self-discipline*" (2 Timothy 1:7).

The next time you find yourself fearful, remember that the same God who was there for the Israelites is there for you and me. Let's continue to recognize our dependence on Him, relying on Him to fight our battles for us. Be strong and courageous!

The Brevity of Life

A good name is better than fine perfume, and the day of death better than the day of birth.

(Ecclesiastes 7:1)

The death rate for humans is one out of one. We will all end up in the grave someday. At seventy-nine years of age, my husband's uncle, Harvey, passed away suddenly. Harvey was out dancing with his girlfriend one night when he started experiencing chest pains. A few days later, he went to the doctor to get himself checked out. The physician found a major blockage in his heart and told him he needed emergency bypass surgery. That day, Harvey was wheeled into the operating room, telling jokes to the doctors as he went. The doctor assured him the surgery would go just fine and that he would come out with flying colors. But Harvey never made it through the surgery; he was gone just like that.

The Bible makes numerous references to the brevity of life on this earth. Psalm 90:5–6 says this:

You sweep men away in the sleep of death; they are like the new grass of the morning—though in the morning it springs up new, by evening it is dry and withered.

Why is it our culture places so much emphasis on youth and beauty? I think it is because most people don't want to face the reality of their own mortality. Death has almost become a taboo subject in our culture. We all want to have this imaginary sense that we will live forever. In reality, this life is like a blip on a radar screen.

For those of us with MCS, many of our physical bodies are wearing out sooner than some folks. As I was thinking about this one day, I realized that ultimately it won't matter whether my body started falling apart at age thirty or age seventy. In the end, for those who know Christ, we are all going to end up with brand new bodies someday anyway. We've got to keep our focus on eternity. The apostle Paul had a unique perspective on death. In Philippians 1:21, he says: *"For to me, to live is Christ and to die is gain."* Now that's a foreign concept to most of us, isn't it?

Having a chronic illness can change our perspective on death. During the time in my illness when I was bedridden for months on end, when I heard of someone who had gone to be with the Lord, I sometimes secretly thought: *They are the lucky one.* To someone who doesn't have a heavenly perspective, this may sound odd. However, if we know Christ, we should look forward to our home going. After all, the Bible does say that the day of our death is better than the day of our birth! Until the time when the Lord calls us home, we should make the most of the life God has given us on this earth. Psalm 90:12 says: *"Teach us to number our days aright, that we may gain a heart of wisdom."*

Today let's enjoy whatever blessings we still have in this life, knowing we will all be home soon!

Emotional Healing

Though my father and mother forsake me, the Lord will receive me.
(Psalm 27:10)

*O*ften the emotional pain associated with MCS is as bad or worse than the physical pain. It breaks my heart as I hear story after story from people with MCS whose friends and families have failed to show love and support toward them in the midst of their illness. Some people with MCS are accused of being mentally ill or attention getters. Those who are too ill to work are sometimes accused of being lazy. I've heard of some families who almost disown their family member with MCS, being embarrassed by their plight. People with MCS sometimes feel like outcasts or modern day lepers, tossed aside by mainstream society.

Stories about lack of accommodation are plentiful. It is common to hear of incidents where family or friends are unwilling to try and do simple favors that may enable a person with MCS to safely attend a wedding, a party, or other type of event. Other times people are willing to accommodate us but do so grudgingly, letting us know how difficult it is. We are sometimes made to feel like we are a burden or that this illness is our fault. Another typical scenario that I hear about occurs when people don't take our needs and requests seriously, and we end up in situations where we become very ill due to the ignorance or lack of compassion and understanding by others. Some people think they can sneak chemical exposures by us and we won't notice. How wrong that assumption is!

When family or friends fail or forsake us in various ways, sometimes the hurt can run very deep and the scars can last a long time. When such painful treatment occurs, where do we turn? Is there any hope for us? The best place I have found to find healing in these situations is through my relationship with Christ. One verse that has ministered to me during times of rejection and brokenness is Psalm 147:3: *"He heals the brokenhearted and binds up their wounds."* What a neat promise to meditate on! Just imagine the Lord applying His balm to your hurting heart and His bandages to your emotional wounds.

Another passage that has encouraged me during periods of deep emotional pain is Psalm 139:17–18: *"How precious to me are your thoughts, O God! How vast is the sum of them! Were I to count them, they would outnumber the grains of sand. When I awake, I am still with you."* Isn't that a beautiful passage? It blesses me to know that God's thoughts about me are like the sand—too numerous to count. It also encourages me to know that He is always with me, every second of the day from the time I wake up in the morning until the time I go to bed at night, even when others have forsaken me.

If you've been hurt by others, receive the Lord's love today. Bask in His love and let Him be your healer. The Great Physician is always available, willing and waiting to bring healing to our deepest hurts and to our broken hearts.

Obedience + Sacrifice = Blessing

⸎

Then God said, "Take your son, your only son, Isaac, whom you love, and go to the region of Moriah. Sacrifice him there as a burnt offering on one of the mountains I will tell you about."

(Genesis 22:2)

*I*n 1988, my husband and I bought our first home on Mercer Island, Washington. After moving in, we discovered it was a very toxic house. One of our neighbors informed us that the home had been a drug lab prior to our occupation of it. In addition, we found out there was a leak in the pipes connected to the oil furnace, allowing toxic fumes to be pumped up into the living space. If that wasn't enough, the home was mold-ridden!

After five years of living in the toxic environment, God provided us a much safer home in Bothell, Washington. What a day of celebration that was! Our home in Bothell had many perks our first house didn't have. It was a fairly new home—about ten years old, it was in a nice neighborhood with curbs and sidewalks, and there were children nearby that my kids could play with. Most importantly, it had no mold, oil leaks, or other chemical exposures that would make me ill.

The day came when I decided to have the carpets cleaned. Still being fairly new to MCS, I wasn't aware of the precautions I should have taken when having this done. After cleaning the carpets, the man we hired applied a toxic air freshener to them. When the job was completed, I entered my home and immediately felt a burning sensation all over my body. In addition, I became disoriented and experienced gastrointestinal problems. I immediately left and went to stay at my parent's home for the night.

After numerous unsuccessful attempts to make our home "safe" for me, we were forced to sell it. Through this experience, I learned that trials reveal what we really love, and I loved my home! I have to admit that I hadn't laid my home on God's altar, giving Him permission to take it if He wished. Looking back, I should've trusted God's plan for my life, even if His plan was different from my own.

In Genesis, we read about the testing of Abraham. God asked Abraham to sacrifice his son, Isaac, as a burnt offering. God tested him to see if he was willing to do whatever He told him to, even if it meant giving up something very dear to him—his own son! Abraham was ready to obey God, and he took Isaac and placed him on an altar. Seeing his obedient heart, God intervened and stopped Abraham from killing him. Afterward, God said to Abraham: *"Now I know that you fear God, because you have not with-held from me your son, your only son"* (Genesis 22:12).

As we learn from Abraham's example, we need to be willing to give up whatever God asks us to. If there is something today that God is asking you to lay on the altar of sacrifice, I encourage you to do it with joy. Genesis 22:16–17 says: *"I swear by myself, declares the Lord, that because you have done this and have not withheld your son, your only son, I will surely bless you."* Just as God blessed Abraham for his obedience, He will bless us for our sacrifices as well.

False Teachings on Healing

You must teach what is in accord with sound doctrine.

(Titus 2:1)

*H*aving lived with a chronic illness for over ten years, one thing that deeply saddens me is the unbiblical teachings within the church on the topic of healing. Along with many others, I have experienced unnecessary guilt and pain due to false teachings. For years I tried to figure out why I hadn't been healed after being prayed for on numerous occasions. *Was it because of my lack of faith? Was it due to sin in my life? Or was it simply because God didn't like me?* I will discuss some of the false notions in regard to healing that are prevalent today, and seek to show from Scripture why these teachings are incorrect.

First, a popular teaching that can be very damaging to people is the idea that if a person has enough faith, healing will occur. The implication is that people can control their destiny in regard to healing simply by mustering up an adequate amount of faith.

The reality is, God is not a genie waiting to grant our every whim simply because we have enough faith. As God of the universe, He chooses if and when to heal people; the decision is not ours to make. The apostle Paul is a great example of a Biblical character that prayed but was not healed of his infirmity. Let's read about his thorn in the flesh:

> There was given me a thorn in the flesh, a messenger of Satan, to torment me. Three times I pleaded with the Lord to take it away from me. Be he said to me, "My grace is sufficient for you, for my power is made perfect in weakness."
>
> (2 Corinthians 12:7–9)

Did God refuse to heal Paul because of his lack of faith? Not at all! Instead, this passage teaches that God promised His power would be made perfect in the midst of Paul's weakness.

Another false teaching that is common today is the idea that sin in a person's life is always the reason for sickness. To be honest with you, in some cases, if people abuse their bodies in various ways such as taking drugs, then sin could be a cause for illness. However, to say that sin is the cause of everyone's illness is simply not true and is certainly not taught in Scripture. The story of Jesus healing a blind man illustrates that sin is not always to blame for a person being sick. John 9:1–2 says:

> As he went along, he saw a man blind from birth. His disciples asked him, "Rabbi, who sinned, this man or his parents, that he was born blind?" "Neither this man nor his parents sinned," said Jesus, "but this happened so that the work of God might be displayed in his life."

Here we see very clearly that the man's blindness had nothing to do with sin in his life. Rather, Scripture teaches that the man was born with an infirmity "so that the work of God might be displayed in his life." God had a divine purpose in allowing the man to be born blind.

When it comes to the issue of healing, the most important thing to remember is that God alone chooses if, how, and when to heal people. He knows the plans and purposes He has in allowing a person to suffer from an illness or affliction. Listen to what God says about His sovereignty:

> *The Lord does whatever pleases him, in the heavens and on the earth, in the seas and all their depths.*
>
> (Psalm 135:6)

There are a variety of reasons people become ill, and only the Great Physician knows the reason for each individual's illness. One reason people get sick is simply because we live in an imperfect, fallen world where viruses, bacteria, and disease exists. Some may become ill from poor lifestyle choices including lack of proper nutrition, rest, and exercise. Others may become sick from chemical exposures that attack various systems of the body. Still others may become ill due to the stress level in their lives or unresolved emotional issues.

Regardless of why we are ill, for those of us who are believers in Christ, we know we will all be healed someday, whether it is in this life or the life to come. Take comfort in that. I Corinthians 15:51–53 says:

> *Listen, I tell you a mystery: We will not all sleep, but we will all be changed—in a flash, in the twinkling of an eye, at the last trumpet. For the trumpet will sound, the dead will be raised imperishable,*

and we will be changed. For the perishable must clothe itself with the imperishable, and the mortal with immortality.

Today if you suffer from a chronic illness and haven't been healed yet, look forward to that day when you will get a brand new body that the Bible promises will be imperishable and immortal!

Banished From Society

I, John, your brother and companion in the suffering and kingdom and patient endurance that are ours in Jesus, was on the island of Patmos because of the word of God and the testimony of Jesus.
(Revelation 1:9)

I have a note posted on the end table next to my bed that says: "MCS is my island of Patmos where God can speak to me." For those of you who have never heard of the island of Patmos, let me explain. The consensus of the early church was that the emperor Domitian banished the Apostle John to the island of Patmos around A.D. 95.[14] During his time of isolation, God revealed to John the prophecies and writings we now know as the book of Revelation.

Many of us with MCS may feel somewhat banished from society. We can no longer participate freely in many activities like we once could. How do we cope with this horrendous predicament? In the midst of our isolation, God can often get our undivided attention. If we let Him, He can accomplish much more in us and through us than He could if we were involved in the hustle and bustle of life. For those of us confined at home much of the time, we can become behind-the-scenes producers and directors. We may not be the "actors on stage" like we once were, but our purpose and usefulness can be equally as great or greater than when we were functioning in mainstream society. There are many ways God can use us from our homes such as prayer, raising godly children, and educating others on the dangers of chemicals.

Recently my husband and I decided to start a family night at our house every Wednesday evening. The purpose will be to develop closer relationships among our family members, as well as to foster the spiritual growth of our children. We will do various projects and games together, as well as have times of prayer and worship. If I didn't have MCS, my husband and I would probably be out leading a Bible study group for adults, and putting our children in the care of a babysitter during that time. There would be nothing wrong with that, but I feel our family night will a positive thing to be able to spend special time mentoring our own children. I believe this is one of many ways God has used MCS in my life to slow me down and spend time on what really counts in life—time with the Lord and with my family.

Earlier, we saw how God used the apostle John's time of isolation to pen Revelation. In addition, several books in the New Testament referred to as "the prison epistles" were written by the apostle Paul during his time in prison. Imagine that God used the isolation of John and Paul to have numerous books of the Bible written!

In the book of Philippians, Paul tells of other positive things that came about as a result of his imprisonment:

Now I want you to know, brothers, that what has happened to me has really served to advance the gospel. As a result, it has become clear throughout the whole palace guard and to everyone else that I am in chains for Christ. Because of my chains, most of the brothers in the Lord have been encouraged to speak the word of God more courageously and fearlessly.

(Philippians 1:12–14)

It's exciting to see how God brought much good out of times of suffering and isolation for the New Testament saints. Today, let's trust God that He has a much bigger, wiser plan than we can imagine to bring glory out of our times of isolation as well.

Storms of Life

The disciples went and woke him, saying, "Lord, save us! We're going to drown!" He replied, "You of little faith, why are you so afraid?" Then he got up and rebuked the winds and the waves, and it was completely calm.

(Matthew 8:25–26)

Have you ever felt like you were going to drown during the challenges of living with MCS? I know I have. After the chemical injury I experienced on an airplane in 1998, my brain was not functioning normally for about nine months. During that time, I experienced focal seizures, where my mind would blank out for a few minutes and I felt like I was in a trance. I was conscious, but was unable to complete a task such as going to get myself a cup of tea. After my mind would come out of the trance-like state, my hands would shake for a few minutes.

In addition to having seizures, throughout this nine-month period I often felt like I do after being exposed to car exhaust—spacey and disoriented. This was a very frightening time for me. To lose control of what was happening to my brain was devastating. I had a hard time remembering things and found it difficult to learn even simple tasks on the computer.

There were many moments and days when I didn't know how I was going to make it through this unbearable ordeal. I was filled with much fear and anxiety. There was no one on this earth who could take away my symptoms, or rescue me from my situation. The only refuge I had was Christ. Psalm 94:18–19 says:

> When I said, "My foot is slipping," your love, O Lord, supported me. When anxiety was great within me, your consolation brought joy to my soul.

I honestly don't know how people make it through MCS without Christ. I am so thankful He is there to be our rescuer, our fortress, and our refuge. Psalm 94:22 says: *"But the Lord has become my fortress, and my God the rock in whom I take refuge."*

If you are feeling overwhelmed by the storms of life today, Isaiah 43:1–3 has this encouragement for you:

> Fear not, for I have redeemed you; I have summoned you by name; you are mine. When you pass through the waters, I will be with you; and when you pass through the rivers, they will not sweep over you. When you walk through the fire, you will not be burned; the flames will not set you ablaze. For I am the Lord, your God, the Holy One of Israel, your Savior.

Aren't those comforting words? Whatever storms you may be facing today, look to Christ to be your refuge. He will be there for you when you feel all alone in your deep trial. God may not protect us from going through storms, but He promises to be there in the midst of them to carry us through.

The Greatest Treasure

For I am convinced that neither death nor life, neither angels nor demons, neither the present nor the future, nor any powers, neither height nor depth, nor anything else in all creation, will be able to separate us from the love of God that is in Christ Jesus our Lord.

(Romans 8:38–39)

I'd like to add MCS to that list—not even MCS can separate us from the love of God that is in Christ Jesus our Lord!

When I was a teenager, there was a Christian rock band called The Brethren. My sister, Cheryl, and I used to listen to them perform at The Sternwheeler, a Christian coffee house in Seattle. One of the vocalists in the group, Wayne Taylor, sang a song by Larry Norman entitled "Can't Take Away the Lord." A couple of lines from the song said this: "You can take away my kids, take away my wife, you can take away my job and you can take away my life. You can take away my house, you can take away my Ford, but you can't take away the Lord."

Isn't that the truth? This earthly life is filled with pain and loss, but the one thing that can never be taken away from us is our relationship with the Lord. One of the tricks Satan uses to try and discourage those of us with MCS is to get us to focus on all the things we've lost since becoming ill. If he can get us to dwell on those losses, we will end up miserable. Instead, we should keep our focus on Jesus:

> *Let us fix our eyes on Jesus, the author and perfecter of our faith, who for the joy set before him endured the cross, scorning its shame, and sat down at the right hand of the throne of God.*
> (Hebrews 12:2)

What have you lost because of MCS—your ability to travel, your career, your friends, your health? Even if our health fails, we still have God's love for us that no one can take away. Psalm 73:25–26 says: "*Whom have I in heaven but you? And earth has nothing I desire besides you. My flesh and my heart may fail, but God is the strength of my heart and my portion forever.*"

God wants to have first place in our hearts. He wants us to know He is always there for us no matter what happens. Regardless of our limitations in life due to MCS, we still possess the greatest treasure on earth—our relationship with Christ. According to 2 Corinthians 4:6–7:

> *For God, who said, "Let light shine out of darkness," made his light shine in our hearts to give us the light of the knowledge of the glory of God in the face of Christ. But we have this treasure in jars of clay to show that this all-surpassing power is from God and not from us.*

Today, let's remember to be thankful for this treasure!

Need a Lift?

If one falls down, his friend can help him up. But pity the man who
falls and has no one to help him up!

(Ecclesiastes 4:10)

One day I was lying on a lounge chair outside on my deck, en-joying the beautiful sunny day. All of a sudden I smelled the stench of pesticides. I quickly ran in the house, closed the windows, and stayed inside for the rest of the day. After being exposed to the pesticide, I spent two days in bed with debilitating fatigue. As I was recovering from that exposure, a neighbor called to inform me he was going to be spraying herbicides that afternoon. Later in the week, when I took my kids to a local schoolyard to ride their scooters, we discovered the grass there had just been fertilized. Because of all the exposures, I spent most of the week sick in bed.

After enduring three pesticide exposures in one week, I was not a happy camper. I was feeling like a helpless victim. Every time I turned around I encountered chemical assaults. I wondered how much longer I could go on living on this toxic planet. I was longing for my heavenly home, telling God He could take me home whenever He was ready. I could relate to the apostle Paul who said:

Therefore we are always confident and know that as long as we are at home in the body we are away from the Lord. We live by faith, not by sight. We are confident, I say, and would prefer to be away from the body and at home with the Lord.
(2 Corinthians 5:6–8)

A couple days later, I regained my energy and was able to attend church. Afterward, our church had a picnic at a local park. At the picnic, I shared with some ladies about my difficult week. I told them how frustrating it was to be assaulted by pesticides against my will. I felt like my week had been stolen from me unnecessarily, as there are many non-toxic methods for weed control and fertilizing available. Life just didn't seem fair.

After that, some of the ladies proceeded to tell me what was happening in their lives. All of a sudden my despair turned to hope. You see, these ladies had challenges in their lives as well. One was a single mother, one was battling cancer, and another had recently undergone major surgery. As I saw them persevering through their struggles with Christ's help, it renewed my courage once again. These ladies helped me turn my focus back on the Lord.

God often uses other people in our lives to lift us up when we are down. In the following verse, we see an example of Jonathan encouraging David in the midst of a very difficult trial:

While David was at Horesh in the Desert of Ziph, he learned that Saul had come out to take his life. And Saul's son Jonathan went to David at Horesh and helped him find strength in God.
(I Samuel 23:15–16)

Are you going through a hard time today? Perhaps you feel like giving up. If so, reach out to a friend or member of the body of Christ for support. Be willing to ask for prayer when you need it. Let a friend give you a lift today.

Godliness

The Lord does not look at the things man looks at. Man looks at the
outward appearance, but the Lord looks at the heart.

(I Samuel 16:7)

Most of us are probably guilty at one time or another of judging people according to outward appearance. Prior to having MCS, I judged people based on external things more than I care to admit. Through the media, our culture teaches us to value beauty and youth. It is very difficult at times to dare to live our lives by different priorities. There is nothing wrong in and of itself in looking our best. The problem comes when we place excessive emphasis on our physical appearance.

Before I became chronically ill, I wore a fair amount of make-up, colored my hair, and made it a priority to look somewhat current and fashionable. Since becoming ill, I have made a pretty drastic turn around. I now wear very little make-up, I no longer color my hair, and I am not consumed with having to wear the latest fashion trends. I still try to look presentable, but I no longer feel like I have to look a certain way to try and impress other people. It has been a very freeing thing for me. I Timothy 2:9–10 says:

I also want women to dress modestly, with decency and propriety, not with braided hair or gold or pearls or expensive clothes, but with good deeds, appropriate for women who profess to worship God.

I now realize the importance of inner beauty, and of focusing my time and energy on becoming the woman of God that He wants me to be. God loves us just the way we are, regardless of our physical appearance. I love the way Psalm 139 describes the special care He took in creating us:

For you created my inmost being; you knit me together in my mother's womb. I praise you because I am fearfully and wonderfully made; your works are wonderful, I know that full well. My frame was not hidden from you when I was made in the secret place. When I was woven together in the depths of the earth, your eyes saw my unformed body.

(Psalm 139:13–15)

Doesn't it bless you to know God uniquely designed each and every one of us? Because of this, we should rejoice in the specific physical characteristics God has given us.

When I was in high school and college, various boyfriends tried to encourage me to join health clubs and spend time working out. It seemed important to them that I have a "buff" body. (I don't claim to have ever achieved that!) There is nothing wrong with exercise and staying physically fit, but an even greater use of our energy is to put our time into eternal goals. I Timothy 4:8 says:

For physical training is of some value, but godliness has value for all things, holding promise for both the present life and the life to come.

Today, I encourage you to spend your time and energy on things that will count for eternity, and accept yourself just the way you are.

Paranoia Vs. Denial

God is our refuge and strength, an ever-present help in trouble. There-fore we will not fear, though the earth give way and the mountains fall into the heart of the sea, though its waters roar and foam and the mountains quake with their surging.

(Psalm 46:1–3)

Living with MCS can make the world seem like an uncertain and scary place, especially to a person like myself who has always thrived on being in control of my life. In 1996, my family was forced to move from the house I loved, due to a toxic air freshener that was applied to our carpets. At the time, I felt like the "carpet had been pulled out from under our feet" in our lives. As a result, I went through a period of intense fear and paranoia. After we moved to a new home in Snohomish, many days I was nervous about stepping outside my front door for fear of what chemicals might be lurking in the air that day. Would it be pesticides, wood smoke, or perhaps the smell of fabric softener drifting from the neighbor's dryer vent?

During this time, I was afraid to touch cats, for fear I would somehow get fleas on me and bring them into my house, necessitating the need for pesticides. At the time I didn't know that non-toxic methods of flea control existed. I feared my new house would somehow get tainted and we would be forced to move again. I was also afraid to walk within thirty feet of my husband's paint barn in the backyard, for fear of what a whiff of paint might do to me. The fear I was experiencing wasn't a normal, cautious fear that MCS sufferers need to have, but an exaggerated fear of the unknown. The lack of being in control of my circumstances drove me to excessive fear.

Along with periods of intense fear, I would vacillate to the opposite extreme, and would go into a denial mode. I would try to forget I had MCS, and would go places without taking precautions for the possibility of chemical exposures I might encounter. I guess I figured if I couldn't be in control of MCS, I would pretend it didn't exist. Real smart, huh?

God finally brought me to a place of balance in my life in the midst of the emotional roller coaster I was on. He showed me the necessity of trusting Him in regard to MCS, and to ask Him for wisdom when I wasn't sure if my fear was excessive or prudent. James 1:5 says:

> *If any of you lacks wisdom, he should ask God, who gives generously to all without finding fault, and it will be given to him.*

The Lord showed me that regardless of what chemical exposures I did unexpectedly encounter along the path of life, I was not to fear, but trust Him. Psalm 34:4 says: *"I sought the Lord, and he answered me; he delivered me from all my fears."* Today, let's trust

God to carry us through the uncertainties involved in our MCS journeys, trusting that He has everything under control, even when we do not.

Are We There Yet?

Now we know that if the earthly tent we live in is destroyed, we have a building from God, an eternal house in heaven, not built by human hands. Meanwhile we groan, longing to be clothed with our heavenly dwelling.

(2 Corinthians 5:1–2)

A common question that children often ask when traveling places with their parents is: "Are we there yet?" Children are often impatient to get to their destination, especially if they're heading somewhere fun like a party or vacation. I know my kids often ask this question numerous times while en route to some type of special event. Sometimes I find myself asking the same question of God in regard to heaven. I ask impatiently, "God, are we there yet?"

One night I attended a Bible study where I was exposed to the fabric softener on someone's clothes. The following day I experienced a chemical depression where no matter what I did, I couldn't seem to pull myself out of it. Fragrances and other chemicals frequently put me in a state of sadness or depression that lasts until my body has had a chance to detoxify them. Often, even if I do all the things that usually help lift my mood, such as reading the Bible, listening to praise music, or calling a friend, I just can't seem to get out from under the cloud of depression.

I think if most of us are honest with ourselves, we wish life were like a fairy tale, where a bride marries her handsome prince and they live happily ever after. Unfortunately, most of us have figured out that this is not the reality of life on this earth. The apostle Paul shares this perspective with us:

> *For while we are in this tent, we groan and are burdened, because we do not wish to be unclothed but to be clothed with our heavenly dwelling, so that what is mortal may be swallowed up by life.*
> (2 Corinthians 5:4)

I appreciate the apostle Paul's honesty about the fact that life on this earth is not always a bowl of cherries, and we should expect to have days where we are just tired of the battle. At times we long to be in our heavenly home with the Lord. We need not feel like failures or inadequate Christians because we struggle with our emotions—it is just the nature of life on this planet.

What can we do when we feel overwhelmed with the burdens of life? When we find ourselves depressed, whether it is from chemicals or not, we need to remember that our feelings are temporary and won't last forever. We must persevere, asking the Lord to help us through the difficult time we are going through. Today, if you find yourself discouraged in the battle of life, continue to reach out to the Lord to be your help in time of need. Psalm 33:20 says: *"We wait in hope for the Lord; he is our help and our shield."*

Priorities

Do not love the world or anything in the world. If anyone loves the world, the love of the Father is not in him. For everything in the world—the cravings of sinful man, the lust of his eyes and the boasting of what he has and does—comes not from the Father but from the world.

(I John 2:15–16)

*T*hose of us with MCS are often confronted with situations that cause us to examine our priorities. In 1997, one of those opportunities occurred in my life. That year my husband and I celebrated our tenth wedding anniversary. We had a very special time as we spent our anniversary night at the Salish Lodge, a beautiful hotel overlooking Snoqualmie Falls. It was a dream come true for us. We had an elegant dinner and enjoyed a relaxing evening afterward.

The following day we decided to do some shopping at a local wholesale warehouse. We found a gorgeous floral couch that we felt would go perfectly in our living room, so I sniffed it to see if I could tolerate it in light of my sensitivities. It appeared to be fine, so we purchased it. Once we moved it into our living room, however, I noticed it had an overpowering chemical smell that I hadn't detected at the store.

My husband and I were both pretty disappointed, but we tried to make the best of it. We decided to store the couch in our garage for a year, hoping it would outgas during that time. After a year, we brought the couch inside our home for a "smell test." Unfortunately, the couch still had a strong chemical odor, so back out to the garage it went. Four years passed, and we decided to bring it in for one last test. Believe it or not, after all that time sitting in our garage, the couch still didn't work for me. Reluctantly, we made the decision to sell it.

Challenges like this that crop up in our lives, test where our true affections lie. At times I still struggle with all the losses that MCS causes in my life—even when it's over unimportant things like couches. When the person who bought our couch hauled it away, it was sad for me, yet a good reminder that material things are not what bring happiness. I must continue to put my affections on things that will count for eternity. Matthew 6:19–21 says:

> Do not store up for yourselves treasures on earth, where moth and rust destroy, and where thieves break in and steal. But store up for yourselves treasures in heaven, where moth and rust do not destroy, and where thieves do not break in and steal. For where your treasure is, there your heart will be also.

If you are facing various losses due to MCS right now, keep in mind that earthly things are temporary. Perhaps you have heard the joke that no one has ever seen a hearse pulling a U-haul trailer. I John 2:17 says: "*The world and its desires pass away, but the man who does the will of God lives forever."* Today, let's remember to keep God's priorities our priorities.

Contentment

My Father, if it is possible, may this cup be taken from me. Yet not as I will, but as you will.

(Matthew 26:39)

It took me several years to accept the fact that I had MCS. For years I tried to cover it up, as I didn't want people to know that I had a physical problem or disability. I wanted so much to be healthy and active, fitting in with the mainstream of life. In the early stages, it was possible to hide my illness. However, as my symptoms grew more severe, I could no longer keep my secret hidden. I was forced to come out of the closet and tell people the truth.

After I started being honest with people, I began enlisting people to pray for me. I had my home fellowship group pray for healing, as well as numerous family members and friends. In addition, I had the elders at my church anoint me with oil and pray. James 5:14 says:

Is any one of you sick? He should call the elders of the church to pray over him and anoint him with oil in the name of the Lord.

After many prayers, I have experienced partial healing over time, yet I still have MCS. What should we do when we've been prayed for more times than we can count, and we are still ill? Personally, I continue to pray for healing. However, at the end of my prayer I always tack on a sentence asking that God's will be done. Jesus was our ultimate example on how to pray during difficult circumstances. Prior to His crucifixion, while praying in the garden of Gethsemane, His prayer was that His Father's will be done.

Whether or not we get healed on this earth is ultimately not going to be that important. All of our earthly bodies are in the process of decay from the time we are born. Ecclesiastes 3:1–2 says: *"There is a time for everything, and a season for every activity under heaven: a time to be born and a time to die."* In the long run, the destiny for all our earthly bodies is the same.

If we keep the long-term perspective in mind, it enables us to accept our illness, make the best of it, and try to find God's purpose in the midst of it. Over the years I have learned to accept my disability, and I do my best to find peace and contentment in the midst of it. I Timothy 6:6 is one of my favorite verses, as it holds an important key to contentment in life. It says:

But godliness with contentment is great gain. For we brought nothing into the world, and we can take nothing out of it. But if we have food and clothing, we will be content with that.

Today, let's work on being content right where God has us, remembering it is up to us to choose contentment regardless of circumstances.

God's Goodness

*One generation will commend your works to another; they will tell
of your mighty acts. They will speak of the glorious splendor of
your majesty, and I will meditate on your wonderful works.*

(Psalm 145:4–5)

*A*fter the chemical injury I experienced in February of 1998,
the Lord showered His goodness upon me in various ways. For a
year after the injury, I was bedridden from sixteen to twenty hours
per day. Because of this, I needed a lot of help to carry out my
duties as wife and mother. The Lord filled in the gaps, providing a
woman who helped drive my kids to school, clean my house, and
take over my part-time job as my husband's office assistant.

Because these various responsibilities were lifted from me, it
allowed me to spend more quality time focusing on my children.
As a result, I was able to develop a closer relationship with them.
What a special gift that was!

Another way the Lord showed His goodness to me during that year was to help me change my view of myself. Prior to the chemical injury, I felt like a failure if I didn't have a lot of energy and wasn't producing a lot. Afterward, the Lord showed me that even if I had to lay in bed the rest of my life and accomplish nothing, God would still love me and value me greatly. My works are not what He's looking for—it's my heart He's most concerned with. 2 Corinthians 12:9–10 says this:

My grace is sufficient for you, for my power is made perfect in weakness. Therefore I will boast all the more gladly about my weaknesses, so that Christ's power may rest on me. That is why, for Christ's sake, I delight in weaknesses, in insults, in hardships, in persecutions, in difficulties. For when I am weak, then I am strong.

Lastly, the Lord displayed His goodness to me that year in the area of friendships. In my time of weakness, the Lord brought several new friends into my life—people who accepted me just as I was. Many of them served me unconditionally, bringing me meals or gifts. Others came over to keep me company when I was having a hard day. Prior to the injury, I used to think people would only want to be friends with me if I was strong and capable. The year after my injury, however, the opposite proved to be true. What a healing thing that was for me!

Trials are a great opportunity for God to show His goodness and faithfulness to us. What a faith builder it is to watch God take care of us in our times of need. Psalm 31:19 says:

How great is your goodness, which you have stored up for those who fear you, which you bestow in the sight of men on those who take refuge in you.

Today, let's recall all the good things the Lord has done in our lives.

A Beautiful Vessel

Then the word of the Lord came to me: "O house of Israel, can I not do with you as this potter does?" declares the Lord. "Like clay in the hand of the potter, so are you in my hand, O house of Israel."
(Jeremiah 18:5–6)

*H*ave you ever wondered how you got MCS? Some people can trace their illness to a specific event or chemical exposure that triggered their symptoms, but many of us don't know exactly how we ended up becoming ill. The first few years after I discovered I had MCS, I wracked my brain trying to figure out what caused it: *Was it the antibiotics I took for acne as a teenager? Was it the moldy home that I had lived in? How about a genetic weakness in my body? Could it have been stress?*

After many hours of contemplating the subject, I finally realized that ultimately it really doesn't matter how I got this illness. The reality is, God is in control of my life. He could've kept me healthy if He wanted, but for some reason He allowed me to become ill. Jeremiah 18:3–4 says this:

*So I went down to the potter's house, and I saw him working at the
wheel. But the pot he was shaping from the clay was marred in his
hands; so the potter formed it into another pot, shaping it as seemed
best to him.*

I love this passage of Scripture. The clay in the hands of the
potter was marred, so the potter decided to shape it into something better. Doesn't this remind you of our lives? The Lord sees
our flaws, and He desires to make us more useful to Him. Through
the trial of living with MCS, God can form us into a more beautiful
vessel if we let Him. Just as a potter knows what he wants to make
out of a lump of clay, so the Lord knows the plans He has for
transforming our lives. Our goal should be to remain moldable in
His hands, allowing Him to mold us into what He desires.

One thing that God has worked on rooting out of my life is
pride—pride in my own accomplishments; pride in the ability to
run my own life; pride in thinking more highly of myself than I
ought to. Pride is a monster that causes so much destruction in
people's lives. I think it is one of the most prevalent sins many of
us struggle with. Proverbs 11:2 says: *"When pride comes, then comes
disgrace, but with humility comes wisdom."*

There are many other areas of my life in which God continues
to change me. Being molded by Him is a lifelong journey.
Philippians 1:6 says:

*Being confident of this, that he who began a good work in you will
carry it on to completion until the day of Christ Jesus.*

Today, let's submit to the loving hand of the Master Potter, letting Him make a beautiful vessel out of our lives.

Bitter or Better?

For I see that you are full of bitterness and captive to sin.

(Acts 8:23)

*I*n 2001, the inspirational story of a man named Jayne appeared in *People Magazine*. Jayne had been diagnosed with ALS, which is a chronic, debilitating illness. At the time of the article, his illness had progressed to the point where he could no longer walk; he had to use a motorized scooter to get around. He could no longer speak, so he had to use a laptop computer outfitted with special software and a voice synthesizer in order to communicate. In the midst of his illness, the stress took its toll on his marriage, so he and his wife separated. In light of all the challenges he faced, at his fortieth birthday party, Jayne said this: "My cross is not greater or lesser than others', only more physically obvious" (*People Magazine* 4/16/01).

What an inspiring attitude! For those of us with MCS, we all have choices to make in our lives as to how we will respond when adversity comes our way. We must decide if we will let difficult circumstances make us bitter or "better." We can choose to be resentful for the hardships that come into our lives, or we can say, "I'm not going to let this ruin my day."

One challenge that has always been difficult for me to handle is when my neighbors spray pesticides. I used to struggle with the fact that I had to leave my windows closed and stay cooped up in the house for four or five days, often during some of the most beautiful days of the summer. I am a person who loves fresh air, and actually needs it physically in order to feel good. In the past, I would let these episodes discourage me. I have learned, however, to take a different approach when my neighbors spray pesticides. Now, even though I may not feel good physically, I try and enjoy my time indoors, spending time with the Lord. I love a quote by Joann McReynold, who said, "Joy is not found in the absence of suffering, but in the presence of God." Sometimes just changing our perspective a bit can help us weather the storms that MCS brings into our lives.

One day at church I had an opportunity to choose whether to become bitter or "better." Since the auditorium at my church had recently been re-modeled, I was unable to go inside the building. My church was very generous to set up a speaker outside so that I could hear the service from the courtyard. On that beautiful sunny day, the birds were singing and the flowers were in bloom—spring was in the air. I was excited to go to church and enjoy the outdoor provision my church had provided. Once I got there, I realized the facility our church met at was in the process of having the exterior of the building painted. At that point, I had a choice to let the roadblock ruin my day or to say, "Okay, God, this circumstance is beyond my control. How do you want me to use my day?" I chose the latter, and went to a local park where I had a fruitful time alone, reading God's Word.

The apostle Paul learned to become "better," not bitter regardless of his circumstances. In Philippians 4:12, he says: *"I have learned the secret of being content in any and every situation, whether well fed or hungry, whether living in plenty or in want."*

Let's not allow the obstacles that come into our lives because of MCS ruin our day. When they come, let's make it our goal to become "better," not bitter.

Simple Pleasures

Give thanks to the Lord, for he is good; his love endures forever.
(Psalm 118:1)

At times, I have felt like MCS is the worst trial imaginable. The reality, however, is that no one escapes from this life unscathed by pain and tragedy. If you take a moment and look at the lives of those around you, I'm sure you will discover that most people have experienced hardships in their lives. Some have dealt with challenges such as cancer, bankruptcy, divorce, or the death of a close friend.

When MCS presents us with seemingly insurmountable difficulties, how do we cope? One thing that has helped me deal with MCS is to learn to appreciate the simple pleasures in life. At the sickest point in my journey, life was simply survival. I had a hard time taking care of even my basic needs. Due to debilitating fatigue, there were many days when it was a challenge just to walk to the kitchen to get myself food. Each day I lived moment to moment.

After being bedridden for months on end, my health slowly started improving. I'll never forget the day when I finally had the energy to go outside and play Frisbee with my son for five minutes. For me, that was a milestone! What a joy it was to be participating in life again, even in a small way. Through that time, I learned to appreciate the simple things that most people take for granted.

Prior to having MCS, I didn't take much time for the simple pleasures in life. The first year after I got married, my husband asked me if I would like to get a bird feeder. At the time I had no interest in such things. I thought: *Who has time to sit around watching birds?* I had places to go, people to meet, and things to do. Fourteen years later, however, after going through the trials of MCS, I have learned how to "stop and smell the roses." I bought my first bird feeder, along with a book on the types of birds that are found in our area. In addition, I have learned to be content reading a book, playing with my cat, or talking with a friend on the phone. I no longer feel the need to be on the go all the time.

Many healthy people are too busy to stop and enjoy the simple pleasures in life. They often run themselves ragged pursuing financial success or admiration in the eyes of others. I think a wise person seeks to live a balanced life. Proverbs 3:13–16 says:

> *Blessed is the man who finds wisdom, the man who gains understanding, for she is more profitable than silver and yields better returns than gold. She is more precious than rubies; nothing you desire can compare with her. Long life is in her right hand; in her left hand are riches and honor.*

This week, let's look for simple pleasures in our lives and praise God for them. It is a great way to lift our spirits. Psalm 146:1–2 says: "Praise the Lord, O my soul. I will praise the Lord all my life; I will sing praise to my God as long as I live."

Why Not Me?

But the needy will not always be forgotten, nor the hope of the afflicted ever perish.

(Psalm 9:18)

Have you ever felt like your life is jinxed since having MCS? I have, and I've talked to many others with MCS who have experienced similar feelings. One of Satan's tricks is to try and make us feel as though God has taken us off His "blessing list." He may try and make us feel that our future is doomed, and that good things only happen to other people. At a point when my health was at an all time low, I felt so hopeless and discouraged that I was basically waiting around for the day when I would get to go to heaven. Looking back, I can see how much I had allowed Satan to beat me down and defeat me. I could relate to the psalmist who said:

My eyes fail, looking for your promise; I say, "When will you comfort me?" Though I am like a wineskin in the smoke, I do not forget your decrees. How long must your servant wait?

(Psalm 119:82–84)

Satan loves to try and cast doubt on the character of God. If he can get us to believe that God is not faithful to His people, we can end up at the bottom of an emotional pit. If we find ourselves in that position, how can we get out? By reading the Word, and believing in God's promises once again. Lamentations 3:21–23 says:

Yet this I call to mind and therefore I have hope: Because of the Lord's great love we are not consumed, for his compassions never fail. They are new every morning; great is your faithfulness.

Recently I found out that my husband will be having surgery soon for diverticulitis. The enemy tried to convince me that my husband will die in the surgery, causing me to be a widow with MCS raising two kids on my own. There is always that possibility, but I do believe God will carry my husband through. According to the surgeon, only about 1 in 10,000 people die from the type of surgery my husband will be having. The enemy loves to get us full of fear, and, as embarrassing as it is for me to admit, for a while I believed his lies. Satan tried to convince me that His promises are for other people, not me. I have now reversed my thinking and am asking myself, *Why not me?* God's promises are for me, and He can work things out for the best. I have had to dig into God's Word, our offensive weapon against the enemy, and start clinging to God's promises once again.

When Satan throws lies at us, we need to look at the truths found in God's Word. God's promises are for all of us who are believers; there are no favorites in His kingdom. The Bible doesn't teach that God is a big mean ogre who wants us to be miserable. Psalm 103:2–5 says:

Praise the Lord, O my soul, and forget not all his benefits—who forgives all your sins and heals all your diseases, who redeems your life from the pit and crowns you with love and compassion, who satisfies your desires with good things so that your youth is renewed like the eagle's.

God doesn't promise that things will always work out how we want. However, if you have had a streak of bad things happen the past few years, do not give up hope for a better future. Believe that God's mercies are new every morning. There is hope ahead for a brighter tomorrow.

Theology of Remembering

I will remember the deeds of the Lord; yes, I will remember your miracles of long ago. I will meditate on all your works and consider all your mighty deeds.

(Psalm 77:11–12)

In the early '80s, I had the privilege of attending Northwest Bible College. In a class called *The Pentateuch,* we studied the book of Deuteronomy. Throughout the semester, my professor, Daryll Hobson, drilled into me a concept I will never forget. He called it "The Theology of Remembering." The idea behind this phrase is that it is very important for believers to remember how God has helped them and worked on their behalf in the past. All throughout the book of Deuteronomy, there are exhortations to remember what the Lord has done. The following verses recall various ways the Lord took care of the Israelites:

He led you through the vast and dreadful desert, that thirsty and waterless land, with its venomous snakes and scorpions. He brought

*you water out of hard rock. He gave you manna to eat in the desert,
something your fathers had never known.*

(Deuteronomy 8:15–16)

We should follow the example set forth in Scripture, making lists of ways God has helped us during challenging times. Following my husband's colon surgery in 2001, I was able to come up with a record of ways God had intervened on our family's behalf during that time. It was so neat to watch God provide for all our special needs. The day of the surgery, our pastor drove my husband to the hospital and prayed with him prior to his operation. Since I was too ill to drive myself, God provided a ride to the hospital for me through my friend, Karen. She kindly stayed with me for nine hours at the hospital during the surgery and recovery time. The week following the surgery, several friends generously brought meals over.

As we recall God's faithfulness to us in the past, it should give us courage to face the present obstacles in our lives, as we remember God's goodness to us. Our family has started a journal where we record different times in our lives where we have seen the hand of God provide for us during various trials. Back in biblical times, the Israelites used to set rocks in certain spots as a remembrance of God's intervention on their behalf. We see an example of this in I Samuel 7:12, which says:

*Then Samuel took a stone and set it up between Mizpah and Shen.
He named it Ebenezer, saying, "Thus far the Lord has helped us."*

I encourage you to start your own remembrance journal of the various ways God has helped you in the past. It's easy for us in the midst of our trials with MCS to lose our faith in God's ability to care for us. As the enemy tries to plant thoughts of worry and fear in our heads, this journal can serve as a visible reminder of God's faithfulness to us in the past. We can then face our future with confidence!

Physiological Fear

You will not fear the terror of night, nor the arrow that flies by day, nor the pestilence that stalks in the darkness, nor the plague that destroys at midday.

(Psalm 91:5–6)

MCS is a very strange condition. One of my friends described it as something out of a science fiction movie. Isn't that the truth? At least for those of us who have had really unusual reactions to chemicals, we can relate to that description. One terrifying reaction I experienced after exposure to jet fuel fumes was physiological fear. It's a hard thing to even put in words, but for several months after the exposure, I had a bad case of irrational fear. I dreaded being alone, and I felt very anxious and paranoid when no one was with me. When I went places, I had an intense fear of exposure to chemicals. At the time, I was so relieved to read about someone else who had experienced similar feelings.

The book I came across was about a painter named Charlie Finch who had been chemically poisoned. In his book *We Won't*

Let You Die, Charlie's experience was described like this: "He had panic attacks, fear of being alone, fear of the night, fear of the unknown, fear that he would never get well. The fear of being alone became great enough that Charlie would cry if he felt that he was going to be left alone."[15] In Charlie's book, he points out how poisons like solvents can affect the mind if the liver is unable to detoxify them properly.

Having symptoms like these can be especially frightening since there are few people who understand the reality of what chemicals can do to our minds. Even doctors who understand and treat MCS often don't tell us about the emotional havoc that can occur as a result of chemical exposures. I'm so thankful the Lord led me to Charlie's book so I knew I wasn't going crazy! A week or two after I was exposed to the jet fuel fumes, I considered having my husband put me in a psychiatric ward. I honestly thought I might be going insane, but my husband was wise enough to know I was not losing my mind—the chemicals were affecting it.

Many times I have taken comfort during my trials as I have read about Job. Evidently he experienced fears of various types in the midst of all his trials. At one point, Job said this to God: *"Withdraw your hand from me, and stop frightening me with your terrors"* (Job 13:21). I'm not sure what the cause of Job's fear or terror was, but it was obvious his fear was intense. Even though he suffered much, Job had the capacity to see light at the end of the tunnel in the midst of what he was going through. Job 23:10 says:

But he knows the way that I take; when he has tested me, I will come forth as gold.

Job trusted that God would take his trial and refine him if he let God work in his life. He knew that God uses the fire of affliction to make us pure and holy.

If you feel like you are in the furnace of affliction today, let God do His work in your life. He is an expert at taking trials and using them for our good and His glory. Like Job, you too will "come forth as gold."

The Best is Yet to Come

We wait for the blessed hope—the glorious appearing of our great God and Savior, Jesus Christ, who gave himself for us to redeem us from all wickedness and to purify for himself a people that are his very own, eager to do what is good.

(Titus 2:13)

In the spring of 2000, my husband and kids took a ten-day vacation to Palm Springs and Disneyland. I stayed home due to the restrictions MCS has placed on my life. It was a difficult time for my family, as we don't enjoy being apart under such circumstances. Since then, we have been brainstorming, trying to figure out ways that would make it possible for us to travel together as a family in the future. One thought we had was to buy a trailer and go camping. As I began to think of all the potential exposures I might encounter, however, I became discouraged. Thinking about neighbors' campfires, barbeques, and bug sprays made me realize there are no easy answers for those of us living with MCS. Sometimes life seems like one big risk!

As often happens when facing the challenges of MCS, my thoughts turned toward heaven. I began imagining the wonderful place where there will be no more trials due to MCS—no more fear of chemical exposures, no more feeling left out as my family goes places without me, and no more isolation due to this illness. I began imagining pure air. Prior to his death, Bill Bright, the founder of Campus Crusade for Christ said he would soon be breathing "celestial air." Isn't that a great word picture?

As believers, I'm so glad we have hope beyond this life. I Corinthians 15:19–20 says:

> *If only for this life we have hope in Christ, we are to be pitied more than all men. But Christ has indeed been raised from the dead, the firstfruits of those who have fallen asleep.*

Because of Christ's resurrection, we are assured the hope of eternal life someday, along with brand new bodies. Imagine an "MCS-free" body. I like that vision! I Corinthians 15:51–52 says:

> *Listen, I tell you a mystery: We will not all sleep, but we will all be changed—in a flash, in the twinkling of an eye, at the last trumpet. For the trumpet will sound, the dead will be raised imperishable, and we will be changed.*

Hallelujah! I can't wait for that day. Revelation 21:4 gives us even more to look forward to: "*He will wipe every tear from their eyes. There will be no more death or mourning or crying or pain, for the old order of things has passed away.*"

Today let's celebrate the hope of eternal life. John 11:25 says: "*I am the resurrection and the life. He who believes in me will live, even though he dies; and whoever lives and believes in me will never die.*"

As my Grandma Ness used to always say, "THE BEST IS YET TO COME!"

A Godly Legacy

Hear, O Israel: The Lord our God, the Lord is one. Love the Lord
your God with all your heart and with all your soul and with all
your strength.

(Deuteronomy 6:4–5)

One advantage of having MCS is that many of us have more time to think than the average person. We often have time to ponder the deep questions of life. Why did God create us? What is the purpose of life? What do we want to be remembered for? Recently, as I was pondering these questions in my own life, I thought about how I want to be remembered after I die. I have thought about this on numerous occasions, and whenever I do, it always serves to help me make decisions about how I want to live my life today. I don't want to live my life haphazardly, but I want to have a sense of direction and purpose. One thing that is of utmost importance to me is that I leave a godly legacy for my descendants.

Despite the limitations MCS can bring into our lives, one very important thing we can do is to leave a godly legacy. It's not what we do in life that counts; our character is what's most important. If you don't have children, you can still have a powerful influence on those around you, whether friends, family members, or neighbors.

In 2 Timothy 1:5, we see the apostle Paul talking about the godly legacy that Timothy's grandmother passed down to her descendants:

I have been reminded of your sincere faith, which first lived in your grandmother Lois and in your mother Eunice and, I am persuaded, now lives in you also.

What a rich spiritual heritage Timothy had! His grandmother, Lois, passed down her faith to her daughter, Eunice, who in turn passed her faith on to Timothy. As believers, this should be our goal as well—to pass our faith on to the next generation. When the time comes for us to leave this planet, we need to pass the torch of faith on to those who are behind us in the journey of life. How do we do this? Deuteronomy 6:6–9 gives us some advice. It says:

These commandments that I give you today are to be upon your hearts. Impress them on your children. Talk about them when you sit at home and when you walk along the road, when you lie down and when you get up. Tie them as symbols on your hands and bind them on your foreheads. Write them on the doorframes of your houses and on your gates.

These verses encourage us to talk about Scripture as we go throughout our day. In addition, we should do all we can to get the Word of God in our hearts. One way I've done that through the years is by posting Scripture verses in various places throughout my home including my bedroom wall, my bathroom mirror, and inside the kitchen cupboards. In addition, I tape Bible verses to the dashboard in my car. By doing this, the verses that are in plain view serve as a reminder throughout the day where my strength comes from. They also help me view my life and circumstances from God's perspective.

Today, I encourage you to think about what kind of legacy you want to leave behind. What can you do to leave a legacy that will be honoring to God? Pray that God will show you how to do this.

Mountain or Molehill?

With your help I can advance against a troop; with my God I can scale a wall.

(Psalm 18:29)

Living with MCS, I often feel like an athlete running around a track, jumping over hurdle after hurdle. The latest challenge I am dealing with is Candida. I have struggled with it intermittently for ten years and feel like I've tried every treatment under the sun for it. I get rid of it for a while, and then it comes back. Last week I hit a point where I was overwhelmed with having to battle it again. After going to a nutritionist, I felt like I was facing a gigantic mountain as I was told to make more dietary changes and try additional remedies. I was dreading the discipline required to stay faithful to the program, and was not looking forward to the possibility of experiencing unpleasant detoxification reactions from the treatments. After thinking about it, I realized that I was blowing my problem out of proportion, and needed an attitude adjustment. Psalm 112:6–8 says:

Surely he will never be shaken; a righteous man will be remembered forever. He will have no fear of bad news; his heart is steadfast, trusting in the Lord. His heart is secure, he will have no fear.

Every time we face obstacles in our lives, we have a choice as to how we will respond. My father's positive attitude whenever he has faced various challenges has been a great example to me. One summer our family was spending time at a cabin on Bainbridge Island, owned collectively by numerous relatives. While my dad and I were outside enjoying the sunshine, my uncle stepped out on the porch and announced in a deeply concerned voice that we had a big problem on our hands. He told us that the old septic tank was showing signs of being full, and no one knew where it was buried. To my uncle, this was a huge crisis. To my dad, however, this was just a minor inconvenience that needed to be dealt with. He had a real "can do" attitude. I will always remember that story, as it is a good reminder that two people can view the exact same situation from totally different perspectives. Our attitude in life is so important.

After recalling this incident, the Lord helped me change my attitude to see my latest Candida battle as a molehill, rather than a mountain. With God on our side, our problems should be minimized, as we trust the Lord to help us. I love the encouragement the psalmist gives in these verses:

In their peril their courage melted away. They reeled and staggered like drunken men; they were at their wits' end. Then they cried out to the Lord in their trouble, and he brought them out of their distress. He stilled the storms to a whisper; the waves of the sea were hushed.

(Psalm 107:26–29)

If you are struggling right now with discouragement, ask the Lord to strengthen your spirit, and help keep your trials in perspective. Ask Him to rescue you from whatever storm you may be going through. He will be there by your side to see you through.

The Holy Roller

Blessed are you when people insult you, persecute you and falsely say all kinds of evil against you because of me. Rejoice and be glad, because great is your reward in heaven, for in the same way they persecuted the prophets who were before you.

(Matthew 5:11–12)

Back in the early '80s, I worked as a waitress at a hotel in Bellevue, Washington. During my lunch break, I would often spend time with the Lord, reading a devotional book or the Bible. One day as I was reading in the cafeteria, one of the waiters I worked with came in, pointed his finger at me, and declared, "There's the holy roller!" He knew he was mocking me, and he probably thought he was really going to hurt my feelings. However, the opposite happened. I felt joy in response to his comment for two reasons. First of all, I knew that God's light was shining through me and people were noticing. Secondly, I knew what the Bible has to say about persecution. The Bible promises to reward those of us who are persecuted for the sake of righteousness.

There are various reasons we may undergo persecution while on this planet. Many of us with MCS have been mocked and insulted as we have stood up for the truth concerning the toxicity of chemicals. Some of us have had to endure verbal assaults while testifying in court in order to obtain disability benefits. Others have had the opportunity to testify for chemical injury trials and have been lambasted by defense attorneys. Whether people take pot shots at our faith, our credibility, or our mental sanity, it's never any fun. Many of us can relate to the psalmist who said:

Have mercy on us, O Lord, have mercy on us, for we have endured much contempt. We have endured much ridicule from the proud, much contempt from the arrogant.

(Psalm 123:3–4)

When we go through times of persecution for whatever reason, it can be helpful to recall the persecution Jesus went through on our behalf. Let's read about how His enemies treated Him prior to His crucifixion:

They stripped him and put a scarlet robe on him, and then twisted together a crown of thorns and set it on his head. They put a staff in his right hand and knelt in front of him and mocked him. "Hail, king of the Jews!" they said. They spit on him, and took the staff and struck him on the head again and again.

(Matthew 27:28–30)

Jesus suffered a lot and was our ultimate example of how to persevere in the midst of being mistreated. We can take great comfort in knowing we are not alone in our suffering. Hebrews 12:3 gives us some encouragement: *"Consider him who endured such opposition from sinful men, so that you will not grow weary and lose heart."*

Today, whatever type of mistreatment you may be enduring, don't lose heart! Receive the comfort of Christ in the midst of your suffering. 2 Corinthians 1:7 says: *"And our hope for you is firm, because we know that just as you share in our sufferings, so also you share in our comfort."*

The Fragrance of Life

For we are to God the aroma of Christ among those who are being saved and those who are perishing.

(2 Corinthians 2:15)

Before having MCS, many of us wore fragrances to make ourselves smell appealing. The truth is that a lot of fragrances contain toxic chemicals that are considered hazardous waste by the E.P.A. Many of these chemicals are the exact same ingredients that are found in solvents used by painters. Because of this, most of us now steer clear of them. Even if we don't wear toxic fragrances anymore, we can still emit a fragrance that is healthy for people—a fragrance the Bible calls "the fragrance of life." This fragrance has to do with spreading the knowledge of God through our lives. Let's read about it:

But thanks be to God, who always leads us in triumphal procession in Christ and through us spreads everywhere the fragrance of the knowledge of him.

(2 Corinthians 2:14)

How do we go about spreading the fragrance of the knowledge of Christ through our lives? One way is to let God's love shine through us by loving people. Each week we should look for ways to bless others. For those of us who are confined at home much of the time, we can either call or send a card of encouragement to someone we know is going through a hard time. Another idea might be to reach out to someone else with MCS by becoming a pen pal or phone prayer partner. There are a lot of ways we can reach out to others in the midst of our circumstances. It just requires a little creativity on our part.

As believers, wherever we go in life, people should be able to detect that there is something different about us through our words and actions. Our mindset should be quite different than those who don't know Christ. We should always be looking for opportunities to share our faith with people, and to minister to them in various ways. If we meet people who are hurting, sometimes offering to pray for their needs is appropriate. We should be emitting the "aroma of Christ" to those we come in contact with. The Bible says we are "the aroma of Christ" among those who are being saved and those who are perishing. 2 Corinthians 2:16 says: *"To the one we are the smell of death; to the other, the fragrance of life."*

If people are open to hearing about God, then our lives will be the "fragrance of life" to them. However, if someone doesn't want to hear about God, the Bible says we are the "smell of death" to that person. A few years back, I was shopping at a clothing store, and I had a chance to share a little about my faith with the sales associate. He seemed interested in hearing about the Lord, and asked me various questions about my faith. On the other hand, his co-worker didn't want to hear anything about Christ. When he overheard me sharing about my faith he said, "I'm getting out of here!" We are not responsible for people's responses to us when we share the gospel with them. All we are responsible for is letting God use us as a vessel to pour out His love and truth to others.

Today, let's pray and ask God to show us ways He can use us to spread the "fragrance of life" to those around us.

Envy Rots the Bones

A heart at peace gives life to the body, but envy rots the bones.
(Proverbs 14:30)

$\mathcal{T}$hose of us with MCS have many opportunities to let the "green-eyed monster" of envy invade our lives. Since many of us have experienced a multitude of losses since becoming ill, it is easy to become resentful and envious of others who we *perceive* have better lives than we do. I stress the word "perceive" because often the things we envy in others aren't things that bring true happiness anyway. The enemy may try and convince us that the grass on the other side of the fence is greener, but the reality is, everyone has problems in life. Often if we knew what others around us were struggling with, we'd prefer not to trade problems with them.

A few years back, I remember watching a Christian television show that often shared testimonies of people who had been healed. I sometimes struggled with envy thinking, *God, it's just not fair! Why do you heal all those other people and not me?* I finally realized that I needed to accept my lot in life, regardless of whether or not it meant I was going to be healed. To continue on in envy and discontent would not be a profitable thing.

In what ways have you been tempted to envy others since having MCS? Perhaps you have been envious of other people who are healthy and don't suffer from chronic health problems. Maybe you have been envious of someone who is better off financially than you, or perhaps you are envious of people with chronic illnesses that have seen great improvement in their symptoms. When we are envious of others, basically what we are saying is that we are not content with the circumstances God has allowed in our lives. Job 5:2 says: *"Resentment kills a fool, and envy slays the simple."*

Now that's a strong warning against being envious of others, isn't it? Some additional verses that warn us against envy are found in Galatians 5:19–21:

> *The acts of the sinful nature are obvious: sexual immorality, impurity and debauchery; idolatry and witchcraft; hatred, discord, jealousy, fits of rage, selfish ambition, dissensions, factions and envy, drunkenness, orgies, and the like. I warn you, as I did before, that those who live like this will not inherit the kingdom of God.*

Notice how envy is listed right along with some of the sins many people consider really serious such as witchcraft and orgies. These verses indicate that envy is not a sin that is to be taken lightly; the consequences can be severe. We all have choices to make in our lives. We can either let envy reign in our lives, which the Bible says will "rot the bones," or we can have a heart at peace, which the Bible says "gives life to the body."

This week, let's choose to sow seeds in our lives that will lead to life, not destruction. Let's not allow envy to infiltrate our thoughts and minds, but let's choose to have a heart at peace.

The Joy of Refinement

Consider it pure joy, my brothers, whenever you face trials of many kinds, because you know that the testing of your faith develops perseverance.

(James 1:2–3)

Alex Rodriguez used to play for the Seattle Mariners baseball team. When the Texas Rangers offered him a contract he couldn't pass up, he accepted it. Upon returning to play in Seattle for the first time after his move to Texas, the fans in Seattle booed Alex when he got up to bat. After the game, a reporter asked him how he handled the negative response from the crowd. Alex replied, "Whatever doesn't break you will make you stronger." Isn't that a great principle for those of us with MCS to keep in mind as we face various challenges?

During my years of living with MCS, I've had some pretty strange reactions after being exposed to chemicals. One day while shopping at a mall, I saw silver spots flashing in front of my eyes.

Another time I experienced temporary blurred vision after going to a massage therapist, due to the oils used. Lastly, after being exposed to ink in a phonebook, I became disoriented. After that experience, I thought, *What kind of a bizarre illness is this where I get spaced out from using a phone book?* Talk about feeling out of control and helpless!

These types of experiences certainly haven't made me feel like I have the world by the tail. On the contrary, they have driven me to my knees. Many times I've had nowhere to turn but to the living God. It is during these times that He has been able to get my undivided attention and do some necessary refining in my life.

When difficulties come, we have two choices. We can either let the trial destroy us or we can let God mature us through it. James 1:4 says: *"Perseverance must finish its work so that you may be mature and complete, not lacking anything."* According to James, we should be joyful when trials come, not because we enjoy the suffering involved, but because we know the outcome of the trial will be for our benefit—to make us "mature and complete, not lacking anything." Once we come to the end of ourselves and our own abilities, it is then that God has the perfect chance to work in our hearts to do the refining necessary to make us pure and holy people.

One way the Lord has been refining me through MCS is to help me realize that my ultimate goal in life should be to glorify God. He has shown me recently that I used to be a very competitive person. Often, society fosters this attitude; we are encouraged to strive to be the best at whatever we are doing. There is nothing wrong with wanting to excel in what God calls us to do, but our ultimate goal in life should be to glorify God, not ourselves. Too often in our society, our lives are spent on our own selfish desires, goals, and ambitions.

Whatever you may be going through today, don't let the trials associated with MCS destroy you. Instead, let them make you a stronger person, more in love with Jesus. Seek to glorify Him with your life. I Timothy 1:17 says: *"Now to the King eternal, immortal, invisible, the only God, be honor and glory for ever and ever. Amen."*

Our True Identity

And God raised us up with Christ and seated us with him in the heavenly realms in Christ Jesus.

(Ephesians 2:6)

$\mathcal{H}$ave you noticed how some people refer to those with MCS as "MCSers" or "EIs?" Personally I feel these labels are a bit degrading. These labels imply that a person is defined by their illness. WE ARE NOT OUR ILLNESS. As Linda Reinhardt, the director of *The Jeremiah Project*, points out, people with other illnesses don't call themselves "Cancers" or "Lupuses." We need to separate our illness from who we are as people. The reality is that we are all people created in the image of God who just happen to have a condition referred to as MCS. Genesis 1:27 says:

> *So God created man in his own image, in the image of God he created him; male and female he created them.*

What an awesome thing to realize we are created in the image of God. Let's look at some further truths we can learn from the Bible about our true identity as believers:

But you are a chosen people, a royal priesthood, a holy nation, a people belonging to God, that you may declare the praises of him who called you out of darkness into his wonderful light.

(I Peter 2:9)

Peter refers to us as a "chosen people," a "royal priesthood," a "holy nation," and "a people belonging to God." We can see several truths about our identity here. First, we see that we are chosen by God and belong to Him. Second, we are referred to as a "royal priesthood." Because of who we are in Christ, we are considered royalty. In addition, we are considered holy, due to Christ's death and the forgiveness of our sins.

Let's look at one more passage that speaks about our true identity. Romans 8:16–17 says:

The spirit himself testifies with our spirit that we are God's children. Now if we are children, then we are heirs—heirs of God and co-heirs with Christ, if indeed we share in his sufferings in order that we may also share in his glory.

Boy, this verse excites me! Here we are referred to as God's children. Once we commit our lives to Christ, we become members of God's family. In addition, we are called "heirs of God" and "co-heirs with Christ." It doesn't get much better than that!

At times, in the midst of our illness, the enemy may try to whisper lies in our ears that we are losers or outcasts. If lies like that come, dispel them with the truths found in God's Word. It is imperative that we understand what our true identity entails—we are created in the image of God, co-heirs with Christ, heirs of God, holy, a royal priesthood, God's children, and a chosen people who belong to God. Now that's a lot to chew on!

Today, let's meditate on these truths and rejoice in our true identity.

One Day At a Time

I am worn out from groaning; all night long I flood my bed with weeping and drench my couch with tears.

(Psalm 6:6)

The strange reactions that can happen to those of us with MCS never cease to amaze me. A couple of years ago, our family got a new toaster oven. I spent several days working to get it outgassed and ready to use. After dinner one night, my husband decided to toast a piece of bread. It was a hot summer evening, and we were sitting out on our deck relaxing. All of a sudden, I heard the toaster "ding," indicating the toast was done. A few seconds later, I smelled something burning in the kitchen. My husband jumped up and ran into the house where he found the piece of toast burnt. Immediately, we opened all the windows in the kitchen area, and in the surrounding rooms. In addition, we turned on five fans and air purifiers full blast. Unfortunately, it was too late; I was already in a reaction from the smoke. So much for the nice romantic time we had been having!

The next morning I woke up, and the kitchen still reeked like smoke. Because of this, I hibernated in my bedroom most of the day. With the fans going full bore throughout the house, it felt like a wind tunnel. My precious son didn't quite know what to do under the unusual circumstances, so he came and hung out with me in my bedroom, watching videos, and looking at his baseball cards. Since I was in a pretty intense reaction, I was depressed and spent much of the day in tears. I could relate to the prophet Jeremiah who said: *"My eyes fail from weeping, I am in torment within"* (Lamentations 2:11). Sometimes I feel so bad that my kids have to go through the trials of MCS along with me, but I have learned to trust that God will use the experiences for good in their lives.

When I'm in the throes of a bad reaction, I often can't think clearly, and I feel overwhelmed, wondering how I will make it through the trials of MCS. During those times, I try to remind myself that tomorrow will be a brighter day, and that my feelings will subside. I know these feelings are common for others with MCS as well. One day my friend Johanna called while she was in a reaction. At the time, she was feeling desperate about her circumstances. One piece of advice I had for her was to put one foot in front of the other.

Sometimes we only have the strength to take the next step in our journey. When we are struggling, we can't worry about how we will make it through tomorrow. All we can do is focus on making it through the day. John 16:33 says: *"In this world you will have trouble. But take heart! I have overcome the world."* God never promised us an easy life, but He did promise to help us through our difficulties. Psalm 91:15 says:

> *He will call upon me, and I will answer him; I will be with him in trouble, I will deliver him and honor him.*

Today, if you find yourself feeling overwhelmed by various hurdles and obstacles in your life, take life one day at a time. Try and follow the advice of Matthew 6:34, which says:

Therefore do not worry about tomorrow, for tomorrow will worry about itself. Each day has enough trouble of its own.

No Pit Too Deep

*Though you have made me see troubles, many and bitter, you will
restore my life again; from the depths of the earth you will again
bring me up. You will increase my honor and comfort me once again.*
(Psalm 71:20–21)

One of my favorite authors is Corrie Ten Boom. She was a wonderful role model, and I have often prayed to become like her.
There are several things that I admire about Corrie Ten Boom—
her love for Jesus, her heart of humility, and the fact that she was a
survivor. Having endured imprisonment in a Nazi concentration
camp, she went on to become a famous Christian author and
speaker. One of my favorite quotes of hers is this: "There is no pit
so deep, that God's love is not deeper still."[16]

Many of us with MCS have experienced depression in varying
degrees. At the lowest point in my MCS journey, I felt as though I
was in a deep pit of depression. During that period in my life, my
husband kept talking about buying a gun for the protection of our
family. I kept pleading with him not to, as there were many mo-

ments during that year when I didn't want to live. I wanted to make sure there would be no method available that might tempt me to end my life. During periods when I was home alone, the enemy would whisper in my ear, "Okay, now is your chance to kill yourself." A close relative of mine had committed suicide, so the enemy would taunt me by saying, "Why don't you do what your relative did?" Fortunately, I always dismissed those horrible thoughts, knowing they came from the pit of hell.

At the time, I didn't have a lot of people in my life who were there to encourage me emotionally; I felt very isolated and alone. When someone is as ill as I was, many people don't know what to do or how to help, so many do nothing. Since I was depressed much of the time, I didn't reach out to people as much as I should have, for fear of dragging them down.

Even though I had little emotional support during that time from people, Jesus was there to carry me through. When we are in a deep pit in our lives, it is important for us to keep our eyes on Him, not on our problems. When Peter was in a boat in the midst of a storm, Jesus came from the shore and started walking on the lake. Jesus asked Peter to walk toward him, so he stepped out of the boat and started walking on the water. As soon as Peter started focusing on the wind and the storm, he began to sink. At that point, Jesus reached out and caught him, saying, *"You of little faith. Why did you doubt?"* (Matthew 14:31)

If you feel as though you are in a deep pit today, put your faith and trust in Jesus. If you take your eyes off Him and start sinking into deep depression, get your eyes back on Him; He will help you through. When all those around us desert us, God is still there to give us the strength to carry on. Psalm 46:7 says: *"The Lord Almighty is with us; the God of Jacob is our fortress."* May He be our strength today. He is our mighty fortress during our times of deepest distress!

The Prone Position

If I must boast, I will boast of the things that show my weakness.
(2 Corinthians 11:30)

In 1993, I started realizing that being exposed to certain chemicals caused me to experience various symptoms. At that point, I had never heard of MCS, and I didn't know anyone else who reacted adversely to chemicals. It wasn't until 1996 that I started learning more about what was happening to me through attending a seminar sponsored by a local physician who specializes in environmental illness. After the seminar, the speaker recommended I join a support group for people with MCS. I took her advice, and, through the group, I met some special people who have become good friends of mine.

Meeting people with similar health problems was such a relief to me. For years, I had been struggling alone as I battled chronic fatigue and the beginning stages of MCS. Before I met anyone else with chronic fatigue, I experienced so much guilt and shame over all the time I spent in bed. I felt like such a failure as I lay in bed day after day, wishing I could be active and enjoying life. I felt so inferior to other people who were out "producing" and "accomplishing" so much. I'll never forget the day when I talked to my friend, Mary, from the support group. When she admitted spending many long hours in bed like me, it was like a huge burden lifted off my shoulders to know that I was not alone! When I call Mary on the phone now, she often chuckles and will tell me she is in her prone position, laying down and resting. This has become a joke between us as we both often assume this position as we chat on the phone.

It took me years to appreciate the value of the prone position, but I have now come to realize there can be benefits to the times of forced solitude many of us experience. In his book *Intimacy with the Almighty*, Chuck Swindoll talks about various disciplines that will help us achieve intimacy with God. Two of these disciplines are silence and solitude.[17] If you think about it, those of us with chronic fatigue are blessed in the sense that we are often given an opportunity to be still before God. So many people are so busy hurrying and scurrying around that they don't take the time to sit before the Lord in silence, reading His Word and listening to His voice. Psalm 46:10 says: *"Be still, and know that I am God."* There are times when we may be laying in bed but are too sick to read the Word of God or pray. That's okay, but during the times when we are able to do so, it is a very valuable way to spend that time.

Jesus encouraged his disciples to take time for solitude. In Mark 6:31–32, He says:

"Come with me by yourselves to a quiet place and get some rest." So *they went away by themselves in a boat to a solitary place.*

During times of solitude, God has a chance to do the necessary pruning in our lives if we let Him. It's a time when God can reveal those areas of our lives that we need to have transformed if we are to become more like Christ. Silence and solitude are not very popular disciplines in our society. Let's take a radical approach, however, and learn to embrace our times of solitude as periods when we can become intimate with the Almighty. There's not a lot more in life that is more important than that![18]

Father Knows Best

Some trust in chariots and some in horses, but we trust in the name of the Lord our God.

(Psalm 20:7)

Recently my cat, Rascal, had an abscess in his cheek. I took him to the vet, who ended up putting a tube in his cheek in order to drain it. Once I got Rascal home, I had instructions from the vet to clean the wound and give him antibiotics. In addition, I was to keep him indoors for several days so that the wound could heal without becoming dirty. For Rascal, who is an outdoor cat, this presented quite a challenge. When I tried to keep him contained in a room he was not familiar with, he meowed, scratched, and went wild trying to get out. As I watched Rascal fighting to get out of his situation, it reminded me of how I have acted during various trials with MCS. Like Rascal, I have frequently kicked, screamed, and fought God's will, thinking I knew better than Him. At times, I have begged God to rescue me from trials associated with MCS.

Since Rascal was fighting so vehemently against his circumstances, I wanted to tell him, "Rascal, I wish you would trust me. I am confining you for your own good. To let you outside right now would not be in your best interest." Of course a cat is not capable of understanding human logic. From a cat's perspective, all he could see was that he was feeling trapped and he didn't like it! When I fight against the confinement of MCS, I know God must want to tell me the same things I wanted to tell Rascal—that He knows what's best for me even when I don't understand, that He loves me, and that my time of isolation has a good purpose. Psalm 25:10 says: *"All the ways of the Lord are loving and faithful for those who keep the demands of his covenant."*

Even when our circumstances are difficult beyond belief, God wants us to trust His character. He is a loving and faithful God who promises to bring good out of any circumstance if we let Him. There is an old hymn entitled "Trust and Obey." One of the lines goes something like this: "Trust and obey, for there's no other way to be happy in Jesus, but to trust and obey." This song talks about two of the most important aspects of the Christian life—trusting and obeying God. We need to develop a childlike faith and trust in our heavenly Father. How do we do this? One way is by getting to know His character and meditating on His attributes. Psalm 9:10 says:

Those who know your name will trust in you, for you, Lord, have never forsaken those who seek you.

The more we get to know who God is, the easier it will be to trust Him. This week let's spend time in God's Word and prayer, seeking a closer relationship with the God of the universe whose love for us is so great our earthly minds have a hard time comprehending it. Psalm 103:8 says: *"The Lord is compassionate and gra-*

cious, slow to anger, abounding in love." Another verse that assures us of the magnitude of God's love for us is I John 3:1: *"How great is the love the Father has lavished on us, that we should be called children of God!"*

As we begin to understand how much the Father loves us, it will be a joy to trust Him, knowing that He knows best.

Peace of Mind

You will keep in perfect peace him whose mind is steadfast, because he trusts in you.

(Isaiah 26:3)

Isn't peace of mind what all of us want? From time to time, I really struggle with keeping my thoughts focused in the right direction. For those of us with MCS who don't live the active lives we once did, this can be a real challenge sometimes; we often have a lot of time to think. Because of this, it is vitally important that we guard the thoughts we allow ourselves to dwell on. Being isolated much of the time can make us vulnerable to letting our thoughts run wild. Satan knows our weaknesses, and he will try and plant all sorts of destructive thoughts in our heads. If we find ourselves thinking irrational thoughts or becoming obsessed with various fears or concerns, how should we cope?

2 Corinthians 10:5 has some excellent advice. It says:

We demolish arguments and every pretension that sets itself up against the knowledge of God, and we take captive every thought to make it obedient to Christ.

In other words, we should immediately discard any thought we have that doesn't line up with the truths and promises found in God's Word. The word "demolish" means: "reduce to ruins; to put an end to; to destroy."[19] We have the power to rid ourselves of those thoughts that come into our minds that aren't beneficial.

Recently, one destructive thought Satan kept trying to plant in my head was the fear that I may have to face surgery someday. Since my husband and father both had surgery in recent months, the topic has been fresh in my mind. As a person with MCS, the thought of surgery is particularly frightening because of so many unknowns. *How would the anesthesia affect me? What would the chemical exposures in the hospital do to me?* I could drive myself nuts with all the "What if?" questions, so I have had to work hard at not letting my mind go in that direction. Ultimately, I have to trust the Lord for whatever happens in my life. If I do have to face surgery someday, then I will have to trust that the Lord will go with me and help me. It doesn't do me any good to worry and fret about something that may never happen. I have been trying to follow the advice of Philippians 4:8, which says:

Finally, brothers, whatever is true, whatever is noble, whatever is right, whatever is pure, whatever is lovely, whatever is admirable— if anything is excellent or praiseworthy—think about such things.

If we could just follow that advice every day, our minds would be filled with peace. Today, if you find yourself becoming obsessed with unhealthy thought patterns, be quick to reject them, knowing they are not from God. Instead, remember to dwell on those things that are true and right. This will bring peace of mind.

Dare to Dream Again

I am still confident of this: I will see the goodness of the Lord in the land of the living.

(Psalm 27:13)

After the chemical injury I experienced on an airplane in 1998, I figured my traveling days were over. I had become so sensitive to chemicals that, for several years, the risks of flying on an airplane or staying in a hotel were far too great for me to take. This past year, however, my family decided that buying a used RV might enable us to have a vacation together again. Recently we ventured out camping, and our trip was a huge success! We stayed at a beautiful campground in La Conner, Washington. It was right on the water, so there was plenty of fresh air. I was able to make it through the trip without any major chemical exposures. What a huge victory it was for me!

At various times during my MCS journey, I have been in situations where I wondered if the "sun" would ever shine in my life again. When I was bedridden and housebound for months on end, I got very discouraged since I had no idea what my future held. *Would I be this sick for the rest of my life? Was there any hope for a better future? Would I feel like a shut-in forever?* I often felt like I didn't have much quality of life. The enemy would whisper lies to me such as: "You will never travel again. Don't count on ever going to the grocery store again. You won't be able to attend church again without becoming ill." Some days I was tempted to believe his lies.

At the lowest point in my MCS journey, I was so sensitive to chemicals that it was difficult for me to go to the grocery store without having a seizure, due to the various chemicals I was exposed to there. As I have gotten healthier though, I now am able to do many things I thought I might never do again. I have been able to go to grocery stores without becoming ill. In addition, I can attend some churches without getting sick. I have also been able to visit people in the hospital without experiencing any adverse reactions. These all have been victories for me.

If you are at a place where you have lost hope for the future, I encourage you to dare to dream again.[20] Dare to believe God has good plans for your life. With MCS, our lives often seem like two steps forward, one step back. We may get very ill for a while, but then regain a certain level of health again. Some of us may not fully recover from MCS, but I encourage you always to keep the hope that things will get better. Even if you have certain restrictions on your life now, it doesn't necessarily mean they will always be there. Psalm 42:5 says:

Why are you downcast, O my soul? Why so disturbed within me? Put your hope in God, for I will yet praise him, my Savior and my God.

Whatever challenges you may be facing today, continue to put your hope in God and His ability to change your difficult circumstances. After all, He is the God of the universe. Jeremiah 32:27 says: *"I am the Lord, the God of all mankind. Is anything too hard for me?"*

Getting Well

*See to it that no one misses the grace of God and that no bitter root
grows up to cause trouble and defile many.*

(Hebrews 12:15)

Many of us with MCS spend a fair amount of time trying to
figure out how we can improve our health. We research various
supplements to see which ones might help. We try different diets
to find those foods that are good for us. We seek medical care from
a variety of practitioners, hoping that one of them will direct us to
some helpful treatments for MCS and other ailments we may have.
All these approaches to improving our health are important. In
addition, however, we must not forget to seek ways to improve our
emotional health.

Our physical and emotional health are connected, and each
one affects the other. If our physical body is ill, it can affect our
emotions. In the same way, if we are experiencing negative emotions, it can cause damage to our physical health. There are many

harmful emotions that can affect our health, one of them being bitterness. If you are struggling with bitterness today, the Bible has some clear advice concerning this topic. Ephesians 4:31 says: *"Get rid of all bitterness, rage and anger, brawling and slander, along with every form of malice."*

That's a pretty straightforward approach, isn't it? Plain and simple, this verse tells us to get rid of it! In other words, get it out of our hearts and lives. I realize that often this is easier said than done. If we are struggling with bitterness towards someone, how do we cleanse our heart of this sin? Ephesians 4:32 tells us: *"Be kind and compassionate to one another, forgiving each other, just as in Christ God forgave you."*

Forgiveness is the key to getting rid of bitterness. The last few years, I have had to work through some bitterness in my own life. I had been holding grudges towards various people for things they did to me years ago that hurt deeply. When I was finally able to forgive the offenders, I felt like a huge burden was lifted off me. When we carry bitterness in our hearts, it can damage our health and weigh us down. In Hebrews, it talks about how allowing a bitter root in our life can cause trouble in our lives. If we want to be healthy emotionally, we must become people of forgiveness and not allow bitterness to pollute our lives.

I know most of us with MCS have felt rejected or misunderstood by others at various times in the course of our illness. It is easy to become bitter when such offenses occur. Is there anyone who has hurt you that you are holding bitterness towards? Perhaps there is a doctor, a former co-worker, a neighbor, a relative, or even a pastor that injured you in some way. If so, ask the Lord to help you forgive that person so you can have peace of mind and heart. Bitterness can sap our energy, so as we get healthier emotionally, our physical health often improves as well.

Today, let's not let bitterness reign in our lives, but let's seek to become people of forgiveness so that we can live the healthiest lives possible.

The Ultimate Goal

Precious in the sight of the Lord is the death of his saints.

(Psalm 116:15)

Cindy Duehring was a hero to many in the MCS community. She was born in Bismarck, North Dakota in 1962. In 1985, while studying to be a doctor, she was poisoned after an exterminator doused her Seattle apartment with pesticides. As a result, she became extremely chemically sensitive, and was forced to live a hermit-like existence. In the midst of her difficult circumstances, Cindy founded the Environmental Access Research Network (EARN). As the director of the organization, she researched medical and legal questions for doctors, scientists, and people with MCS from around the world. In addition, she received Sweden's Right Livelihood Award, which is known as the alternative Nobel Prize (*People Magazine* 2/9/98). After fighting her illness bravely for fifteen years, Cindy passed away in June 1999.[21]

Cindy Duehring was a beautiful, talented Christian woman who died at the age of thirty-six. We know God could've chosen to heal her, but for reasons beyond our human comprehension, He allowed her to die an early death. The amazing thing to me is that even though she had one of the most severe cases of chemical sensitivity I have ever heard of, she also did more to help further the cause of the chemically injured than anyone else I know. This sparks the question in my mind as to whether or not physical healing should be our ultimate goal in the midst of having MCS.

The first few years I had MCS, I wanted to be healed so bad! I couldn't fathom having to live the rest of my life with this insidious condition. After years of living with this illness, however, I finally decided I better make the best of my situation, as I didn't have any guarantee I would ever be healed while on this earth. One day while a missionary to India, Dan Bushy, was home on furlough, I asked him how people should respond if they pray for healing and don't get healed. I love Dan's response. He replied, "People shouldn't put their hope in healing, but should put their hope in God!" Isn't that a great answer? In Cindy's case, it could be that God used her life for His purposes more in the few years she had on this earth, than if she had lived a long, healthy life. It's not really how long we live that's important, it's what we do with the years we have that counts.

If you are very ill and may not live a long life, don't fear death. I love how Pastor Robert Case describes the death experience for believers. When people in our congregation die, he says that they have graduated to their heavenly home. Doesn't that perspective help take the fear out of death? I Corinthians 15:54–55 says:

When the perishable has been clothed with the imperishable, and
the mortal with immortality, then the saying that is written will

come true: "*Death has been swallowed up in victory.*" "*Where, O death, is your victory? Where, O death, is your sting?*"

Whether or not you get healed of MCS while on this earth, I encourage you to make the most of the years God gives you. Each day should be cherished and lived for God's glory. Ephesians 2:10 says:

For we are God's workmanship, created in Christ Jesus to do good works, which God prepared in advance for us to do.

Where is God?

Will the Lord reject forever? Will he never show his favor again? Has his unfailing love vanished forever? Has his promise failed for all time?

(Psalm 77:7–8)

Where is God? I have asked this question on numerous occasions during my MCS journey. Often when circumstances seem bleak, God appears to be silent. Back in 1996, my family was forced to evacuate our home because a toxic air freshener had been applied to the carpets. After staying with relatives for a few months, we ended up moving to a hotel for four months. During that time we had no idea what was ahead. There was a possibility we might be able to get the house safe for me again, but we weren't sure if that was a realistic possibility. If not, we would be forced to sell our home and find a new one.

During that episode in our lives, I remember feeling very forsaken by God. Two years earlier the Lord had delivered us out of a toxic home on Mercer Island and had provided what I considered a "safe," dream home in Bothell. Now, it appeared that my home was being taken away from me. I could not figure out why God would allow this, and He wasn't revealing any answers to me. It seemed like a cruel joke. I felt like Job who said:

> But if I go to the east, he is not there; if I go to the west, I do not find him. When he is at work in the north, I do not see him; when he turns to the south, I catch no glimpse of him.
>
> (Job 23: 8–9)

In addition to our housing dilemma, I had concerns about my health. I noticed my chemical sensitivities becoming gradually worse, and I feared ending up like those I had met with MCS who were practically hermits. At the time, I was still living a fairly normal, active lifestyle. I couldn't imagine the thought of being stuck at home most of the time. In a desperate frame of mind, I asked my friend Sarah one day: "What will I do if my chemical sensitivities get worse?" Sarah responded: "God is testing you. Will you still love Him, trust Him, and serve Him even if your health gets worse?" That was not what I wanted to hear, but I knew Sarah was right. 2 Samuel 22:2–3 says:

> The Lord is my rock, my fortress and my deliverer; my God is my rock, in whom I take refuge, my shield and the horn of my salvation. He is my stronghold, my refuge and my savior.

The Lord wants to be our fortress during times of trouble. *The American College Dictionary* defines fortress as: "any place of security."[22] When God appears to be silent, He wants us to place our security in Him. No matter how deep our pain or how intense the crisis, God wants us to trust Him, knowing His will is best. He is always one step ahead of us, charting the course He has mapped out for our lives. Job 13:15 says: *"Though he slay me, yet will I hope in him."* Whatever you may be going through today, continue to put your hope and trust in Him.

After the Storm

"For my thoughts are not your thoughts, neither are your ways my ways," declares the Lord. "As the heavens are higher than the earth, so are my ways higher than your ways and my thoughts than your thoughts."

(Isaiah 55:8–9)

Many times after a crisis in our lives, a time of blessing follows. After staying in a hotel for four months during our carpet crisis, we were unable to make our home "safe" for me again. Through a series of events, however, we started to see Gods' plan for us unfold.

For twelve years my husband had been involved in a business partnership, and through being forced to evacuate our Bothell home, the Lord led my husband to terminate his partnership. He also led us to sell our dream home in Bothell and purchase a new home in Snohomish. Both these decisions turned out to be very good ones for us. Being a sole proprietor in his business, my husband's income level increased substantially. In addition, the home we were able to purchase in Snohomish was twice the size of our Bothell home, and was on a much larger piece of property. Having the extra property turned out to be much better for my health, as we now have a greater cushion from the various toxins that can drift from our neighbors' properties.

Even though it took us awhile to see God's plan for us, in His time He did show us the good that came out of our time of crisis. God supplied for us in so many ways during our difficult time. He provided an insurance settlement for us that covered the cost of our hotel stay. In addition, He provided an unexpected loan, which enabled us to purchase our home in Snohomish. Watching God's faithfulness and provision was amazing! He is a good God who can be trusted no matter what we are going through. After our trial was over, God encouraged me with this verse:

> *For you, O God, tested us; you refined us like silver. You brought us into prison and laid burdens on our backs. You let men ride over our heads; we went through fire and water, but you brought us to a place of abundance.*
>
> (Psalm 66:10–12)

Are you going through some type of storm today? Is your faith being tested? Do you wonder if God is still there for you? If so, I encourage you to continue to put your faith in Jehovah Jirah, your provider, who cares for you more than you can imagine! Our lives are like a tapestry. We may only see the backside that looks like a tangled mess, but God sees the front side—the beauty of what He is doing in and through our trials. Psalm 100:5 says: *"For the Lord is good and his love endures forever."*

Today, let's continue to trust God and believe in His goodness and love as we look forward to the blessings that come after the storm.

Codependency

You shall have no other gods before me.

(Exodus 20:3)

Codependency has become quite a buzzword during the past few decades. We hear psychologists everywhere talking about it. June Hunt, in her book, *Healing the Hurting Heart,* describes it this way: "Codependency is basically a relationship addiction. It is usually characterized by a weaker, dependent person who feels the *need to be connected* to a stronger person, while the stronger person feels the *need to be needed.* In reality, both people are insecure. What began as a constructive, joy-filled relationship results in a destructive cycle of manipulation and control that saps the joy and happiness out of life."[23]

When a person is in a codependent relationship, there is often an unhealthy dependency on a person rather than on God. This occurs as the person seeks to get the needs for love and security met in the wrong place. According to June Hunt, this type of dependency is modern-day idolatry and should be confessed before God as sin.[24]

How can we break free of these types of destructive patterns in our relationships? First, we shouldn't allow other people to manipulate us. When we let people control us, it can sap our energy. Many of us with MCS also suffer from chronic fatigue, and we can't afford to let others rob us of our limited resources.

Second, if you have a tendency to control or manipulate others, stop doing it. A healthy relationship involves a mutual respect for the needs of the other person. Codependent people often have their own selfish interests at heart. They attempt to demand their way through pouting, crying, silence, or cruelty. We need to rely on God to be the true source of getting our needs for love, security, and significance met. It is not fair to expect any one person on this earth to meet all our needs. 2 Peter 1:3 says:

> *His divine power has given us everything we need for life and godliness through our knowledge of him who called us by his own glory and goodness.*

The book of Ephesians talks a lot about the spiritual riches we have because of Christ. Listen to Ephesians 3:16–19:

> *I pray that out of his glorious riches he may strengthen you with power through his Spirit in your inner being, so that Christ may dwell in your hearts through faith. And I pray that you, being rooted and established in love, may have power, together with all the saints, to grasp how wide and long and high and deep is the love of Christ, and to know this love that surpasses knowledge—that you may be filled to the measure of all the fullness of God.*

I encourage you to let God's love fill your life to overflowing. As you move out of codependent patterns in relationships, you will be healthier emotionally. As you break the chains of codependency in your life, you will be amazed at how free you will feel.

The God of All Comfort

Scorn has broken my heart and has left me helpless; I looked for sympathy, but there was none, for comforters, but I found none.
(Psalm 69:20)

As I journey along the path of living with MCS, at times I get weary of the experience of rejection, which seems all too common in our lives. The holidays are a time when I especially feel like an outcast. Most of the time I don't try to attend holiday parties, but choose instead to stay isolated at home. The few times I do step out and ask for accommodation, I find mixed reactions. On some occasions I am met with kindness and compassion above and beyond what I could've imagined, yet other times the treatment I receive is hurtful at best.

When people are kind and compassionate, I am very grateful. However, when I ask for accommodation only to see people sigh and roll their eyes at me, it makes me wish I had never bothered to ask. It makes me feel like it would be better to stay home in seclusion. People like that often feel their party is ruined if they are not free to enjoy their scented products such as candles, potpourri, or perfume. At times when I have attended parties where the hostess has treated me with disdain, I have felt like a party wrecker. On numerous occasions, people have confessed to me that they have become physically or emotionally exhausted from trying to accommodate me. This certainly does little to brighten my day. At times like that, I try and imagine how people like that would cope if they had to face the challenges those with MCS deal with day in and day out. Treatment like that makes me empathize with the psalmist David who said this:

> I am a dread to my friends—those who see me on the street flee from me. I am forgotten by them as though I were dead; I have become like broken pottery.
>
> (Psalm 31:11–12)

Have you ever felt like that—like broken pottery? At times when I feel like this, I sometimes wonder how to ease the pain. Where can I go to find the compassion and comfort I so desperately desire? 2 Corinthians 1:3–4 says:

> Praise be to the God and Father of our Lord Jesus Christ, the Father of compassion and the God of all comfort, who comforts us in all our troubles, so that we can comfort those in any trouble with the comfort we ourselves have received from God.

When those around us reject us or treat us like we are a burden, the Father of compassion and the God of all comfort promises to be there to pick up the pieces of our broken heart. We are never a burden to Him, and He always welcomes us with open arms. Psalm 69:33 says:

The Lord hears the needy and does not despise his captive people.

Today, if you are feeling rejected by friends, loved ones, or the church, run into the loving arms of our Heavenly Father. He will be there to wrap His arms of love around you and give you the true, lasting comfort only He can give. I praise God for His comfort in times of need!

Thirsting For God

I said to the Lord, "You are my Lord; apart from you I have no good thing."

(Psalm 16:2)

$\mathcal{I}$n 2002, on Memorial Day weekend, the Lord blessed me with a special outing. On Saturday morning, my family drove a few hours away to a quaint Bavarian town nestled in the mountains called Leavenworth. We walked through some gift shops and stopped for a drink at Starbucks, our favorite coffee shop. After exploring a few more tourist spots in the area, we headed back over the mountains toward home. As we reached the town of Skykomish, we saw a cute motel overlooking a rushing river. We decided to stop and see if there might be a room that would work for my chemical sensitivities. The innkeeper showed us one, and, lo and behold, it worked for me! There were no detectable chemical odors in the room—even the sheets and towels had no fragrance on them. I was so excited as I felt this was a small miracle. In the past four years, the two occasions that I had tried staying in motels I had become ill from mold or chemicals.

Once we checked into the motel, we drove about twenty miles to try and find a restaurant for dinner. All we could find were smoke-filled diners, so we ended up stopping at a grocery store and getting ingredients to make deli sandwiches. We made the best of the situation and had a fun picnic in our motel room. After having my family go on many vacations without me, it was great to be able to be together again. It brought me so much joy to see my kids excited to be able to go on a trip where their mom could finally join in on the fun!

On Sunday morning we went out for breakfast. The restaurant was a "hole in the wall," but the food was great. The carpet and benches looked like they hadn't been updated in about forty years, but at least there was no brand new carpet outgassing! It was a bit like going back in time since the furnishings looked like they were from the '60s. After breakfast we headed back to our motel, and I spent the next few hours enjoying a time of serenity by the river. I was able to spend some time reading my Bible and worshipping the Lord as I sat on the grassy riverbank. While watching the river rushing by, I thought of the following verses:

> *As the deer pants for streams of water, so my soul pants for you, O God. My soul thirsts for God, for the living God.*
>
> (Psalm 42:1–2)

The verses reminded me of a song entitled "As the Deer," so I sang it as I enjoyed the beautiful scenery. I had a very sweet and special time with the Lord and was so thankful for the time of refreshment.

No matter where we are, we can experience times of worship and communion with the Lord. Colossians 1:16 says: *"All things were created by him and for him."* God created us for the purpose of having an intimate relationship with Him. Today, let's spend quality time worshipping and getting to know Him.

Rejoice Always

Rejoice in the Lord always. I will say it again: Rejoice!
(Philippians 4:4)

We all have important choices to make every day about how we will respond to our circumstances and losses in the midst of MCS. Often times it's tough to keep our attitude right when things don't turn out how we'd like. In the mid '90s, my parents bought a condo on a beautiful golf course in Palm Springs. After their purchase, my parents extended an invitation to all their children to come visit them each winter. Not being able to pass up such a wonderful opportunity, I made it an annual event for three winters in a row to go down there to soak up the sun and get refreshed. To me, it was like paradise. While visiting one year, I heard one of the senior citizens who live there call it "God's waiting room for heaven."

Following the chemical injury I had on an airplane in 1998, I have not been able to go down there anymore. Initially, it was a difficult adjustment for me. During the cold, dreary winter months,

I would watch various family members including my husband, my kids, and my siblings' families fly down to Palm Springs one by one for a vacation. I was happy for them, but wished I could go as well.

One day during my devotions, I read Philippians 4:11, which says: *"For I have learned to be content whatever the circumstances."*

My first thought was, *Lord, am I supposed to be content even if I can't go to Palm Springs this year?* I felt like the Lord was saying to me, "Yes, Janine, even if you can't go to Palm Springs." That was a hard thing for me to come to grips with, but I finally realized that the Lord was right. The only way I was to have peace was to accept my circumstances even when they weren't what I would've chosen for my life.

Fanny Crosby was a very famous hymn writer who wrote over 2,000 hymns. She became blind as a baby after an eye infection, which was improperly treated by a man claiming to be a physician. Fanny's attitude in the midst of her disability astounds me. When she was eight years old, she wrote the following poem:

"Oh, what a happy child I am,
Although I cannot see!
I am resolved that in this world
Contented I will be!

How many blessings I enjoy
That other people don't!
So weep or sigh because I'm blind,
I cannot—nor I won't."[25]

Fanny Crosby appears to have grasped the apostle Paul's exhortation to rejoice in the Lord always, not because of difficult circumstances but in the midst of them. The apostle Paul wrote the book of Philippians from prison, and even from his prison cell, Paul was able to find joy in his relationship with the Lord. If we continually seek peace that comes from our circumstances, we will never be happy.

Today, let's make it our aim to rejoice even in the midst of difficulty, as we praise and glorify Him with our lives.

A Life Well Lived

For he has clothed me with garments of salvation and arrayed me in a robe of righteousness.

(Isaiah 61:10)

What constitutes a life well lived? This question is one all of us have most likely grappled with at one time or another. Christina Sollenberger is one woman with MCS who has inspired me as I have observed the strength of character she has displayed while living in difficult circumstances. Christina and her husband, George, have spent nine of the last twelve years living in a travel trailer due to their inability to find other safe housing for Christina. They have no well to get water from, so they must drive into town where they get water to haul onto their property. To bathe they take sponge baths, and for cooking, Christina uses two hot plates and a small convection oven.

Many of Christina's clothes have holes in them and some are threadbare. Finding safe clothes is a challenge for her because when she has tried to purchase new ones, she has been unable to tolerate them even after cooking them in a pressure cooker and washing them many times. She recently resorted to borrowing some of her husband, George's, shirts and pajamas. Thankfully, he has a good sense of humor about this and thinks they look cute on her. During her times of frustration over her lack of suitable clothing, Christina focuses on the fact that someday when she gets to heaven she will be clothed with garments of righteousness.

Over the years, Christina has endured her share of hardships in regard to her health situation. In the early '80s, she contracted valley fever that required complete bed rest. By 1984, she was so ill that she and George started planning her funeral. Fortunately, the Lord led Christina to a medication that helped her regain a certain measure of health, and it turned out her time on this earth was not up yet. God still had more plans for her.

How has Christina survived all the ups and downs of her battle with MCS? One way she has coped is by clinging to God's Word. One of Christina's favorite Scriptures is Isaiah 30:15, which says: *"In quietness and trust is your strength."* When Christina becomes frustrated and discouraged by her circumstances, God often reminds her of this verse, telling her to quiet down, read Scripture, and trust His sovereignty. When she does this, God fills her with peace and gives her strength to go on.

Even though Christina's health limitations have prevented her from realizing many of the dreams and aspirations she had as a young woman, she realizes that a successful career and worldly acclaim are not what counts in God's economy. What matters to Christina is fulfilling God's purpose for her life, no matter how great or small the calling. Christina realizes the importance of trusting God every step of the way in her difficult journey in life. She looks forward to the day when she will receive her transformed body and hopes she will hear her Master say: *"Well done, good and faithful servant!"* (Matthew 25:21) That will be the mark of a life well lived!

The Value of Prayer

You will seek me and find me when you seek me with all your heart.
(Jeremiah 29:13)

In the spring of 2001, some friends of our family, the Albrights, were looking for homes for their new kittens. We decided it would be fun to adopt one, so we went over to their home to pick one out. Once we got there, however, the kittens were so cute and irresistible that we ended up bringing home three of them! We named them Rascal, Sapphire, and Angel. After about a month, Angel disappeared, so we were left with two kittens. As they grew, the two remaining cats had very different personalities. Rascal needed a lot of attention and loved to be held, but Sapphire was fiercely independent. She would disappear all day, and, if we were lucky, she might come home at night to be tucked into her cat condo. She never let us hold her, but would quickly squirm out of our arms if we tried.

One fourth of July we went camping, and boarded our cats at a nearby kennel. Somehow one of our cats pried open the window in the room where they were staying. Both cats escaped by jumping out of the two-story window. Rascal was missing for three days, and was then found by a lady who had volunteered to search for the cats. Sapphire, on the other hand, was missing for thirty-eight days before she was located. A woman found her meowing in a ditch one day, weak and dehydrated. We were excited to get the phone call from her that Sapphire had been found.

Once we took Sapphire to the vet, we were told that three of her paws were dislocated or fractured. She was a mess and had to have surgery on her two front paws. After her long recovery, I noticed a distinct personality change in Sapphire. Our once independent cat had now become very needy, longing for our love and affection. I feel a lot closer to Sapphire now than I did prior to her injuries, simply because we spend much more time together than we used to.

The change in my relationship with Sapphire reminds me of what can happen to those with MCS. Before becoming ill, many were very independent, and may have been too busy to spend much time with the Lord. Going through hard times, however, has driven many to their knees. I've talked to numerous people with MCS who now take much more time out of their day to pray and seek the Lord than prior to their illness. These people have developed a very special relationship with Him as a result of the time spent in His presence. Proverbs 15:8 says: *"But the prayer of the upright pleases him."*

God delights in our prayers, and the more time we spend in His presence, chances are, the more we will become like Him. J. C. Ryle said: "What is the reason that some believers are so much brighter and holier than others? I believe the difference in nineteen cases out of twenty, arises from different habits about private prayer. I believe that those who are not eminently holy pray *little*, and those who are eminently holy pray *much*."[26]

Today, I encourage you to deepen your prayer life, spending more time talking to God and letting Him speak to you. Doing so will help you become more like Christ.

No Pity Needed

So it will be with the resurrection of the dead. The body that is sown is perishable, it is raised imperishable; it is sown in dishonor, it is raised in glory; it is sown in weakness, it is raised in power; it is sown a natural body, it is raised a spiritual body.

(I Corinthians 15:42–44)

$\mathcal{D}$ave Roever is a man who has reason to suffer from self-pity, but, instead, he has been a wonderful example of courage in the face of tragedy. In the late '60s, Dave served in Vietnam as a member of the Brown Water Black Beret in the U.S. Navy. On July 26, 1969, a grenade exploded six inches from his face. Dave was severely burned, and was scarred beyond recognition. His wounds nearly cost him his life, but with the support of his loving wife by his side, Dave recovered from his injuries. Even though he is severely disfigured, he has gone on to minister in various ways throughout the years to adults and youth alike.[27]

Back in the '80s, I had the privilege of waiting on Dave Roever one evening when he came in for dinner at a restaurant where I worked. I'll never forget how the love and joy of the Lord shone through on his face. His joyful attitude in spite of all he's been through in life really impressed me. Over the years, as I've watched Dave on television, his sense of humor has also been an inspiration to me.

To be honest, at times the challenges of MCS have been so overwhelming that I have struggled with self-pity. During those periods, it was a challenge not to complain to others about my problems. When I was going through a really difficult time a few years back, I had a friend who e-mailed me and said, "How are you doing, other than the struggles with your health?" That question made me realize our conversations had become lopsided, as it appeared to my friend that all I talked about was my illness. In order to have healthy friendships, I discovered that I needed to discuss topics other than my health—things like my relationship with the Lord, current events, special memories of my life before I became ill, as well as hopes and dreams for the future.

I think it's very important that we have friends who can listen to our struggles, share our burdens, and pray for us. This is a vital part of coping with a chronic illness. Galatians 6:2 says: *"Carry each other's burdens, and in this way you will fulfill the law of Christ."* I have benefited greatly from being involved in local and Internet support groups for those with MCS. The emotional and prayer support I have received from the new friends I have met through these groups is invaluable! I do need to seek balance, however, and be careful not to excessively burden others with my problems. As I get the support I need from people, I try to avoid seeking pity from them. I Corinthians 15:19 says:

If only for this life we have hope in Christ, we are to be pitied more than all men.

If this earth were all we had to look forward to, we would have a lot of reasons for self-pity. Fortunately, someday these earthly bodies will be traded in for heavenly ones with no more sickness or pain. Focusing on that should give us hope and strength as we persevere until the day we see Jesus face to face. Let's look forward with great anticipation to that day.

Dealing with Anger

But now you must rid yourselves of all such things as these: anger,
rage, malice, slander, and filthy language from your lips.

(Colossians 3:8)

Since having MCS, I have talked to many people who have admitted to me that they have become angry after enduring various
types of chemical poisonings. Some people get angry at pesticide
companies or the government. Others I've spoken with have experienced anger toward law enforcement agencies for allowing meth
labs to continue poisoning them in neighboring apartments. God
made us emotional beings, and it is normal for us to experience a
wide rage of emotions, including anger. Let's look at a few things
we can learn from the Bible about this topic.

First of all, anger itself is not a sin, as the Bible is full of examples of people who have experienced anger. It's how we handle
it that is important. There are numerous occasions in Scripture
where Jesus himself displayed anger. In Matthew 23, a few of the

names He called the Pharisees were "hypocrites, snakes, brood of vipers, and whitewashed tombs." In another passage, we see Jesus in the temple area overturning the tables of the moneychangers, and the benches of those selling doves. In both these situations, Jesus expressed anger when he saw sinful attitudes and actions taking place.

David is another example of someone in the Bible who is seen expressing anger. Throughout the psalms, David vented his anger and frustrations honestly. Listen to his cries to the Lord:

> *Fierce men conspire against me for no offense or sin of mine, O Lord. I have done no wrong, yet they are ready to attack me. Arise to help me; look on my plight! O Lord God Almighty, the God of Israel, rouse yourself to punish all the nations; show no mercy to wicked traitors.*
>
> (Psalm 59:3–5)

God can handle our honesty. In the passage above, David showed his anger as he asked God to "punish all the nations" and "show no mercy to wicked traitors."

If we are angry due to a situation where we feel violated, it's helpful to express it to God and ask Him to deal with our enemies. In addition, we should pray for those who have hurt us. If we do these things, we can release our feelings of anger and not live in a continual state of being upset, as the Bible encourages us not to let the sun go down on our anger:

> *In your anger, do not sin: Do not let the sun go down while you are still angry, and do not give the devil a foothold.*
>
> (Ephesians 4:26–27)

If you find yourself getting angry about some circumstance in your life, commit the situation to the Lord. Let Him vindicate you, and He will be your refuge and fortress in times of trouble. Psalm 59:9 says: *"O my strength, I watch for you; you, O God, are my fortress, my loving God."*

Finding Rest in His Word

You are my refuge and my shield; I have put my hope in your word.
(Psalm 119:114)

The first significant chemical exposure I recall having occurred in 1993 after we had our condo painted with a highly toxic oil enamel. At the time, I experienced chest pains, fever, chills, gastrointestinal problems, depression, and anxiety. It was a very difficult time for me as I was new to the whole concept that chemicals could make a person sick. The clinical ecologist I tried to make an appointment with had a two-month waiting list, so that was a further source of frustration. At the time, God was my only refuge, since I had no one to give me any answers for what was happening to me. I asked the company we bought the paint from if the product used to paint our condo could make a person ill. I was assured by one of the employees that the damage done by exposure to the product would be no worse than the results of drinking a beer. It wasn't until much later I found out how wrong that statement was!

For several months after the paint exposure, I experienced anxiety attacks since the paint had affected my nervous system. I reached out for help to Suzanne Dull, a woman that I knew had experienced anxiety attacks due to hormonal fluctuations. I asked her for advice on how to cope with what I was going through. Her counsel to me was to dig into the Word of God and memorize it to find solace during my times of anxiety. I took her advice, and started memorizing Psalm 91. After several weeks, I had memorized most of the chapter, and I recited it when the waves of anxiety would come. When I meditated on God's Word, He filled me with His peace. Psalm 91:1–2 says:

> *He who dwells in the shelter of the Most High will rest in the shadow of the Almighty. I will say of the Lord, "He is my refuge and my fortress, my God, in whom I trust."*

God is a master at bringing good out of hard times if we let Him. The anxiety I experienced from the paint exposure drove me into the arms of Jesus and His Word, where I found rest. I wrote verses down on note cards and read them often in order to get them planted in my memory. A verse that comforted me greatly during that time was Psalm 91:4:

> *He will cover you with his feathers, and under his wings you will find refuge; his faithfulness will be your shield and rampart.*

This week no matter what you are facing, I encourage you to dig into God's Word. Let Him speak to you, giving you His peace and rest. Try to memorize a verse here or there if you are able, so that you will have verses ready to recall in times of need. If you are too ill to read or memorize the Word of God, consider getting the Bible on cassette tapes to listen to, or tune in to hear Bible teachers via the radio or television. There is great solace to be found in His

Word! Psalm 119:28 says: *"My soul is weary with sorrow; strengthen me according to your word."*

Enjoy Each Day

This is the day the Lord has made; let us rejoice and be glad in it.
(Psalm 118:24)

Several years ago, Pastor Marty Anderson encouraged his congregation to enjoy each day as a gift from God. At the time, his son, Jeremy, had Juvenile Rheumatoid Arthritis. On numerous occasions, Jeremy had to be put in the hospital for pericarditis, which is where the sack around the heart fills with fluid. This condition can be very serious, and even life threatening at times, but thankfully, God restored Jeremy's health after each incident.

The reality of life is that none of us knows how long we will be on this earth. My father-in-law, Stan, once said something that really hit me: "All we know is that we are all here today. We don't know what tomorrow holds." He is so right! James 4:14 says:

Why, you do not even know what will happen tomorrow. What is your life? You are a mist that appears for a little while and then vanishes.

In light of this, how should we live our lives? The Lord has impressed upon me the importance of living life one day at a time. So often worry has been like a vice grip, holding me in its clutches. In the past, I have spent way too many hours worrying and fretting about the future, letting the "what if" questions plague me. *What if my health gets worse? What if my husband dies? What if there is no one to care for me in my old age? What if there is no "safe" place for me to live when I get older?* Isaiah 46:4 contains this promise:

> *Even to your old age and gray hairs I am he, I am he who will sustain you. I have made you and I will carry you; I will sustain you and I will rescue you.*

Worry is the opposite of trust. Matthew 6:25–27 says:

> *Therefore I tell you, do not worry about your life, what you will eat or drink; or about your body, what you will wear. Is not life more important than food, and the body more important than clothes? Look at the birds of the air; they do not sow or reap or store away in barns, and yet your heavenly Father feeds them. Are you not much more valuable than they? Who of you by worrying can add a single hour to his life?*

Rather than spending our time worrying about the future, we should put our trust in God. Psalm 62:8 says: *"Trust in him at all times, O people; pour out your hearts to him, for God is our refuge."* Psalm 108:4 has this encouragement about God's character: *"For great is your love, higher than the heavens; your faithfulness reaches to the skies."*

Today, let's not give in to the temptation of worry. Instead, let's enjoy each day on this earth as a special gift from the Lord, knowing that God is one step ahead of us in taking care of tomorrow.

Do Not Lose Heart

If only my anguish could be weighed and all my misery be placed on the scales! It would surely outweigh the sand of the seas.

(Job 6:2–3)

$\mathcal{I}$t's very sad to me that there is still so much ignorance about the fact that pesticides are poison. Because of this, many people continue to use them on their yards, having no idea the depth of pain and suffering they may be inflicting on people who live around them. This week after several of my neighbors sprayed pesticides, I was really struggling with discouragement, feeling very ill, and not knowing what long term damage might be done to my health as a result of the unwanted chemical exposures. In the midst of my reaction to the pesticides, I picked up my Bible and started reading about the apostle Paul's trials. In 2 Corinthians, Paul says this:

I have worked much harder, been in prison more frequently, been flogged more severely, and been exposed to death again and again. I have labored and toiled and have often gone without sleep; I have known hunger and thirst and have often gone without food; I have been cold and naked.

(2 Corinthians 11:23,27)

Reading about what Paul went through gave me comfort to know that I am not alone in my trials. Many other saints through-out the ages have also endured times of painful suffering. If we expect to have a rosy journey on this earth, we will be in for a big disappointment. Jim Elliot was a famous missionary who had the kind of perspective we need to have in order to make it through the overwhelming difficulties MCS can bring into our lives. Jim Elliot felt called to go preach the gospel to a remote tribe of people called the Auca Indians in Ecuador. While attempting to minister to them, he and four other missionaries were murdered by the very people they were trying to reach with the love of Jesus. Jim Elliot gave his life for the cause of Christ. He was willing to lay down his life if that is what it took to be obedient to God's plan for him. A famous quote of Jim's is: "He is no fool who gives up what he cannot keep to gain what he cannot lose." You see, Jim was not concerned about what happened to his earthly body. He knew that what mattered most was how his life counted for eternity.

If we are to persevere through trials with joy and hope, we need to have the same eternal perspective Jim Elliot had. People on this earth can damage our health or kill our bodies, but they can't kill our souls! No matter what happens to us on this earth, we will ultimately triumph someday when we get our eternal re-wards. 2 Corinthians 4:16–18 says:

Therefore, we do not lose heart. Though outwardly we are wasting away, yet inwardly we are being renewed day by day. For our light and momentary troubles are achieving for us an eternal glory that far outweighs them all.

If you are discouraged today, don't lose heart. We have an eternal hope that no one can take away and will far outweigh anything we endure on this earth. Praise the Lord for the hope we have in Him!

God's Approval Alone

As a bridegroom rejoices over his bride, so will your God rejoice over you.

(Isaiah 62:5)

$\mathcal{B}$ack in the early '90s, before I had a diagnosis for my illness, I had a painful visit with an internist. At the time, I was searching desperately for a doctor who could tell me what was wrong with me and what I could do about it. I had read books on chronic fatigue and Candida, and happened to mention this to the internist. After listening to my health problems, he told me in a very cold tone that he was sorry, but I would have to find another physician. The only thing he could recommend for me was anti-depressants. He told me that there was no one in his practice that believed Candida could cause health problems. I went away devastated, feeling very misunderstood and rejected. I got the impression that he saw me as a crazy, emotional woman whose illness was all in her head.

All throughout our lives, we may encounter people who will criticize us, judge us, or make us feel rejected. How should we respond when others hurt us? Galatians 1:10 gives us some excellent advice when it says:

> *Am I now trying to win the approval of men, or of God? Or am I trying to please men? If I were still trying to please men, I would not be a servant of Christ.*

According to this verse, we should care what God thinks, not man. If we are secure in His love for us, then there is no need to be discouraged when people are rude or reject us. We can let the attacks roll off our backs and not take them to heart. Our aim should be to please God and seek His approval alone. I Corinthians 13:5 talks about some of the characteristics of love:

> *It is not rude, it is not self-seeking, it is not easily angered, it keeps no record of wrongs.*

If someone does something offensive to us whether it is related to our illness or not, this verse exhorts us not to get easily angered or offended. It's so easy to be touchy, but if we allow ourselves to be that way, we hurt others and ourselves. If we want to experience peace in our lives, we need to learn to have godly responses when we are unjustly treated.

Joseph was a great example of someone who endured a lot of mistreatment throughout his life yet never became bitter. At one point his jealous brothers sold him into slavery. Surprisingly, Joseph didn't hold a grudge against them for this. Instead, many years later, he actually helped save them from a famine by providing food for them; he learned to show love even to those who were abusive toward him. What a great role model he was!

Like Joseph, we should not keep a record of offenses that have been perpetrated against us. If we do this, we will be able to live in peace and not let bitterness gnaw away at us. It will help us experience emotional freedom. Today, let's seek to be secure in God's love for us and seek His approval alone in our lives.

The Bread of Life

It is written: "Man does not live on bread alone, but on every word that comes from the mouth of God."

(Matthew 4:4)

For many years, Mary Russell enjoyed a thriving career in the banking industry. In her spare time Mary enjoyed golf, tennis, skiing, photography, and painting. In addition, she traveled abroad to places such as Egypt, Europe, Hong Kong, and Thailand. In the early '80s, however, Mary's life began to change as she started to experience some unexplained health problems. Over the next few years, she gradually became aware that things such as natural gas, car exhaust, tap water, and formaldehyde were making her sick.

In 1985, Mary saw a flyer at a health food store about environmental illness, which led her to see a physician who specialized in the field. It was then that Mary finally realized that she was chemically sensitive. Since that time, her health has deteriorated to the point where she is severely restricted as to the places she can go.

It's been over fifteen years since Mary has been able to enjoy going to the movies, the opera, or even restaurants, as going to these places poses too great of a risk of chemical exposure for her.

All of the restrictions on Mary's life have forced her to reorder her priorities—faith, family, and friends are now what are most important to her. Having been stripped of so many of the pleasures she once enjoyed, Mary now chooses to spend a good deal of her time reading God's Word. In the last couple of years Mary has read the whole Bible through from cover to cover. She is currently in the process of reading it in its entirety for the second time. These days, Mary seeks spiritual nourishment from God's Word.

John 6:35 says: *"I am the bread of life. He who comes to me will never go hungry, and he who believes in me will never be thirsty."* In this verse, Jesus refers to Himself as the "Bread of Life." He says that anyone who comes to Him would never be hungry again. What He is referring to here is not physical hunger but spiritual hunger. If we commit our life to Jesus, then He promises our spiritual hunger will be satisfied. As a result, we will not need to look for satisfaction anywhere except through our relationship with Christ.

Psalm 119:71 says: *"It was good for me to be afflicted so that I might learn your decrees."* Mary feels that the Lord used her affliction with MCS as a catalyst to bring her close to Him. Through contacts made at her physician's office, she slowly became aware of her need to get to know God better. She says that sometimes her faith is the only thing that gets her through the day. Like Mary, many of us have also drawn closer to the Lord through our affliction with MCS.

This week, let's remember to thank the Lord for the good that He is doing in our hearts through our trials with MCS. Let's look to the "Bread of Life" to satisfy our deepest needs.

Give Up Control

Therefore, I urge you, brothers, in view of God's mercy, to offer your bodies as living sacrifices, holy and pleasing to God—this is your spiritual act of worship.

(Romans 12:1)

*A*re you a control freak? I know I can be. If most of us are honest with ourselves, we prefer to be in charge of our lives, making decisions about our destiny. A few years ago, the facility where my church met refinished the floor in the main auditorium with a highly toxic oil-based product. Because of that, I was no longer able to attend services. I had no idea how long it would take for the floors to outgas to the point where it would be safe for me to go inside the building again. I knew there was a possibility it could be a few weeks, a few months, or perhaps even as long as a year or two. Since there was no way to predict when it would be, I wondered what God wanted me to do next. I wasn't sure if I should stay home on Sundays or find another church to go to temporarily or permanently.

How should we respond when unexpected curve balls come into our lives? Sometimes I take a mature approach and immediately think, *Okay, Lord, I trust you in this, knowing your plan is best for me. I accept this trial as coming to me filtered through your loving hands.* Other times, though, I kick and scream, thinking: *Oh, please God, no! This isn't fair! Please fix the situation quick!* One barometer of our spiritual maturity is how we respond to situations when we are not in control. The more mature we are spiritually, the quicker we will accept whatever circumstances God has allowed in our lives.

MCS can be a great instrument for God to use in order to help us learn to give Him control of our lives. Those of us with MCS never know when the next trial will hit us, and we will once again be faced with the question, *Now what, God?* During times like these, we need to lay our lives on the altar of sacrifice, being ready to give up our hopes and dreams. We must be willing to accept God's plan for us, whatever it may be. It's not always easy, but it is necessary if we are to experience God's peace in the midst of the uncertainties of life. Romans 12:2 says:

> *Do not conform any longer to the pattern of this world, but be transformed by the renewing of your mind. Then you will be able to test and approve what God's will is—his good, pleasing and perfect will.*

The world says, "Take control of your life. Go after what you want and you will get it." God's way says, "Give me control of your life. I know what is best for you. My will is good, pleasing, and perfect." Psalm 119:75 says: *"In faithfulness you have afflicted me."* God is faithful to permit problems and afflictions in our lives that He knows will help make us into the people He wants us to be.

Today, I encourage you to make it your goal to truly offer up your life as a living sacrifice. Don't hop off the altar, but let God have His way with you.

You Are a Tool

As iron sharpens iron, so one man sharpens another.

(Proverbs 27:17)

MCS frustrates those of us who have it, but it also creates challenges for those around us. The other day I came across a prayer journal my daughter had started when she was about eight years old. In it, she wrote the following request: "For mom to not have a illniss cuse it is driving me crasy." Another example of how my family has been challenged by my health condition occurred recently. My son was scheduled to go to summer camp, and I was planning to make the three-hour trip with my husband to drop him off. At the last minute, I decided not to go since I had just endured three days of migraines due to various fragrance exposures; I knew my body needed to rest. When I told my husband about my change of plans, he replied, "That's okay. It'll be easier to relax if you're not along." What he meant by that comment was that he wouldn't have to go through the hassle of protecting me at every turn from the various chemical exposures I might encounter along the way.

When I see how my illness hurts and affects my family, it makes me feel sad, and, at times, I feel like I'm a burden to them. When I experience these types of feelings, I try and remind myself that God can use the situation as a tool for good in their lives if they let the Lord refine them through it. One lesson I've seen the Lord teach them in the midst of my illness is how to serve. Mark 10:45 says: *"For even the Son of Man did not come to be served, but to serve, and to give his life as a ransom for many."* Even though it hasn't always been easy, through the years my husband has served me relentlessly during the ups and downs of MCS. He's driven me to doctor appointments, brought me take-out meals when I was too tired to cook, and done the grocery shopping for years on end. What a gift he has been to me!

Another lesson I've seen the Lord teach my family is to put aside their own desires for my benefit. Philippians 2:3–4 says:

> *Do nothing out of selfish ambition or vain conceit, but in humility consider others better than yourselves. Each of you should look not only to your own interests, but also to the interests of others.*

Those of us with MCS are very aware of how much the people around us have to sacrifice in order to accommodate our special needs. Our family members are not always willing to make these sacrifices for us, but when they do it is a special gift.

One last lesson I've seen the Lord teach my family through living with someone with MCS, is to be content with a simple life. Because of my illness, we have chosen not to do very many up-grades to our home or its furnishings. We have learned that happiness is not found in having the current trends in colors or styles in our home.

The next time you start feeling like a burden to your family or those around you, focus on the fact that God can use your trial of MCS to develop qualities such as compassion, unselfishness, and love in their lives. Pray that those around you will be open to the work God wants to do in their lives through your situation.

Never Say "Never!"

I will sing of the Lord's great love forever; with my mouth I will make your faithfulness known through all generations.

(Psalm 89:1)

My husband and I have been married for seventeen years, and we have often enjoyed sneaking away for our anniversary to stay in a hotel by ourselves without the kids. For several years I was unable to stay in hotels due to my severe sensitivities. At one point, I gave up hope that I would ever again be able to have a special getaway with my husband. On our fifteenth anniversary, though, the Lord blessed us with a trip to the Doubletree Inn in Bellevue, Washington, for three nights. That particular hotel holds many special memories for us, as we met there in 1986. At the time, I had worked as a waitress, and Dean, who is now my husband, was a regular customer. As I waited on him, we chatted and got to know each other a bit. We eventually started dating and the rest is history.

As a testimony to the Lord's goodness, I'd like to share a few highlights from our fifteenth anniversary celebration He provided for us. We set out for our trip on July 18, the date of our anniversary. We checked into the hotel in the late afternoon, and after being in the room about ten minutes, I heard a knock at the door. The hotel management had sent us a complimentary bottle of sparkling cider and some gourmet chocolate chip cookies. What a special touch that was! We really felt they rolled out the red carpet for us.

That evening we went out for an early dinner, and were able to enjoy a nice meal on the Seattle waterfront. We made it through dinner without any problems from fragrances or other possible chemical exposures. After dinner we decided to take a walk down by the water on Alki Point. As we were walking along, we saw a man spraying what we thought might be pesticides. My husband said, "Honey, I think I see a tank—run!" So I donned my charcoal mask and we both started running like lightning towards our car. As we got close to the car, however, we realized the man simply had a garden hose and was watering his flowers. Boy did we have a good laugh over that one! Once we realized there was no danger, we resumed a romantic walk along the waterfront.

The following three days we enjoyed all sorts of fun activities—swimming, shopping, and fine dining. The Lord protected me from chemical exposures wherever we went. What a joy it was to feel like my old self during that time. During one of our meals out, my husband made the comment, "Janine is back!" What he meant by that was that I was able to do a lot of things on that trip that I never dreamed I'd be able to do again. I praise God for all the things He is allowing me to do that I never thought possible. Psalm 13:6 says: *"I will sing to the Lord, for he has been good to me."*

Sometimes in our MCS journeys, it may seem like there are many things we will never do again. If you are feeling like that, take heart. Never say "never!" You don't know what good plans God may have ahead for you. Keep the hope that things will look up.

You Are Precious!

Since you are precious in my sight, and because I love you . . .

(Isaiah 43:4)

$\mathcal{H}$ave you ever felt like God didn't care about you? I'm sure many with MCS have felt that way at one time or another—I know I have! After having MCS for about three years, I started feeling bitter towards God. I didn't turn my back on Him or anything, but I felt like He had deserted me. During that time, a girlfriend confronted me in love, asking me if I had put a shield around my heart, preventing God from getting close to me. I had to admit she was right, as I had been keeping God at a distance. I didn't sense His love for me since I was interpreting love in all the wrong ways. I erroneously thought that if God loved me, then He would only allow positive circumstances in my life. After all, how could a loving God allow me to suffer so much?

Through the years, I have gained a greater understanding of God's love. I don't understand it perfectly by any means, but I now know that He loves me more than I could ever possibly imagine, even when He allows trials to occur in my life. There are many passages in the Bible where God talks about His people in endearing terms. In Deuteronomy 32:10, God says this about the people of Israel:

> He shielded him and cared for him; he guarded him as the apple of his eye, like an eagle that stirs up its nest and hovers over its young, that spreads its wings to catch them and carries them on its pinions.

Imagine that! God refers to those He loves as "the apple of his eye." This verse talks about the fact that God's love for His people is similar to that of an eagle protecting its young. Try to visualize, for a moment, God hovering over you like a mother eagle hovering over its babies. Isn't that a comforting picture? Just like a mother eagle catches its young when they fall, God is there to be with us during times of trouble.

Growing up, none of us experienced perfect love from our parents, as they were only human. Only God's unconditional love for us is perfect. Many of us have a hard time comprehending His love since we've never experienced that kind of love from anyone on this planet. I love a quote from Chuck Smith about God's love. He says this: "To know that He is for us, and that He loves us, is the greatest source of security any person will ever know."[28]

I recommend you pick a few verses from Scripture that talk about God's love and meditate on them, asking God to show you how precious you are to Him. I pray that you will begin to grasp the magnitude of His love for you. Romans 5:8 says: *"But God demonstrates his own love for us in this: While we were still sinners, Christ died for us."* It encourages me greatly to know that God loved me so much that He sent His own son to die for my sins. John 15:13

says, *"Greater love has no one than this, that he lay down his life for his friends."* There is indeed no greater love than that!

The Testing of Our Faith

We are not trying to please men but God, who tests our hearts.
(I Thessalonians 2:4)

*W*hy does God allow trials in our lives? One person I have found to have a meaningful perspective on this question is a pastor by the name of Jon Courson. Jon pastored a church in Oregon for many years called Applegate Christian Fellowship. I have had the opportunity to hear Jon speak at several pastors' conferences, and he truly is an inspiration. Jon has been through some very deep trials in his life, yet he has maintained his love for the Lord and has had a godly, heavenly perspective in the midst of his challenges.

The first deep loss Jon experienced was the death of his first wife. As he and his wife were driving up to the mountains one day to go skiing, their car hit some ice, spun around, and ended up wrapped around a redwood tree. Jon miraculously survived, but his wife didn't make it through the accident. Eventually Jon remarried, but his trials were not over. He lost a second member of his family, as his teenage daughter was killed in a car accident early one morning on her way to school. In light of all that Jon has gone through, what advice does he have for others going through trials? Why does God allow tragedies to occur?[29]

Jon sees trials as tests. When we are tested by trials in life, they illuminate what is really in our hearts. Just like a piece of fruit that is squeezed reveals what is inside, so trials reveal what we are really like. Deuteronomy 8:2 says:

> *Remember how the Lord your God led you all the way in the desert these forty years, to humble you and to test you in order to know what was in your heart, whether or not you would keep his commands.*

This verse refers to the fact that tests shed light on what is in our hearts, and whether or not we will continue to obey God even when things in our life go sour. Trials reveal where our hope lies. If our hope is in things of this world, we will be devastated when bad things happen. However, if we are setting our sights on heavenly things, then we can approach our problems from a godly perspective.

Jon Courson points out that the tests God gives us are open book tests. We have the Word of God as our guide to tell us how to respond to the difficulties in life. In addition, Jon reminds us that we have a tutor, the Holy Spirit, who is available to help guide us through our trials. Jon believes that God always painstakingly prepares us for tests. Anything God allows in our lives, He has prepared us to face and will be with us through it.

As trials come into our lives while living with MCS, let's face them with confidence and perseverance, knowing God will be there to see us through. Let's not lose our faith or hope in the God who made us, but let's follow the advice of Hebrews 10:35 which says:

So do not throw away your confidence; it will be richly rewarded. You need to persevere so that when you have done the will of God, you will receive what he has promised.

Remember, it's only a test![30]

What is My Ministry?

There are different kinds of gifts, but the same Spirit. There are different kinds of service, but the same Lord. There are different kinds of working, but the same God works all of them in all men.
(I Corinthians 12:4–6)

In 2000, I was able to attend church regularly with few problems from chemical exposures. In December that year, however, the facility where my church met did some remodeling. All of a sudden, I was no longer able to attend the church that had been "safe" for me, so I ended up staying home alone on Sundays. Being the social person that I am, it turned out to be a very depressing time for me. I felt like a caged bird—a bird that had been let out for a while to fly and sing, but was suddenly locked up again. What a horrible feeling! I wondered why God allowed this to happen to me. After all, how could God use me when I was "locked in a cage?"

Most of us with MCS experience times of isolation. Some of us can relate to the psalmist who said: *"I am like a desert owl, like an owl among the ruins. I lie awake; I have become like a bird alone on a roof"* (Psalm 102:6–7). At times, we may wonder: *How can God use me in the midst of my seclusion?* We may question how we can make a positive difference for God while living on this planet.

If you think having a ministry in the midst of living with MCS is an impossible dream, I would like to challenge you to change your thinking. Many of us have adopted the false notion that in order to be used by God, we need to be involved in a formal ministry position such as a worship leader, Sunday School teacher, or missionary. The truth, however, is that our ministry is as simple as living out the Christian life in our sphere of influence. We are all ministers simply because we know and serve Christ. Bruce Wilkinson, in his book, *The Prayer of Jabez,* says this: "Our God specializes in working through normal people who believe in a supernormal God who will do His work through them. What He's waiting for is the invitation. That means God's math would look more like this:

My willingness and weakness
+ God's will and supernatural power
= my expanding territory."[31]

If you desire to have more of an impact for Christ in this world, pray that God would bring people along your path that He would like to minister to through you. Acts 20:24 says:

However, I consider my life worth nothing to me, if only I may finish the race and complete the task the Lord Jesus has given me—the task of testifying to the gospel of God's grace.

Whatever your circle of influence, let God use you right where you are.

Everything to Gain

The fool says in his heart, "There is no God."

(Psalm 14:1)

*H*ow do we know there's really a God who created the universe and who has a purpose and plan for our lives? When chronic illness hits us, the enemy may try and convince us that there is no God. He may try and whisper in our ear that if there were a God, he wouldn't allow us to suffer so much. At times when I've had such thoughts enter my head, I've been forced to re-evaluate why I believe in God. Romans 1:20 says:

> *For since the creation of the world God's invisible qualities—his eternal power and divine nature—have been clearly seen, being understood from what has been made, so that men are without excuse.*

According to this verse, it should be obvious to us that there is a God simply by looking at creation. This verse says that having seen all God has made, we have no excuse for not believing in Him. If you try and imagine that all the scientific mysteries in our world came about as the result of a big bang of some sort, it really does seem ludicrous. For me, it's much easier to have faith in the fact that God created the universe, rather than believing a random explosion is responsible for it all.

What will happen if those who believe in God are wrong at the end of their lives? My grandfather, Henry Ness, said that if there turns out to be no God, believers in Christ have nothing to lose. They'll just die and turn back to dust. However, if they are right in believing there's a God, then they will have everything to gain—eternal life with Christ! On the other hand, for those who don't believe in God, they will have everything to lose. When you look at it that way, the decision to believe or not believe in God seems obvious.

As you go about your daily life, I encourage you to notice the wonder and marvel of God's creation. Psalm 19:1–4 says:

The heavens declare the glory of God; the skies proclaim the work of his hands. Day after day they pour forth speech; night after night they display knowledge. There is no speech or language where their voice is not heard. Their voice goes out into all the earth, their words to the ends of the world.

Don't you love those verses? It's as if God's creation is shouting to us about the glory of God through the beautiful trees, flowers, mountains, animals, oceans, and other beautiful aspects of His creation. That gets me excited about the greatness of God—about His majesty, His awesome power, and His dominion over the earth. As you enjoy the beauty of God's creation this week, let it be a reminder of why you believe and have committed your life to the true and living God of the universe. If you haven't made that commitment yet, I encourage you to do so. Remember, in doing so you will have everything to gain!

Ignorance isn't Bliss

Defend the cause of the weak and fatherless; maintain the rights of the poor and oppressed.

(Psalm 82:3)

As I talk to people in the MCS community, some have had positive experiences in getting churches to accommodate their special needs, while others haven't been so fortunate. Some feel hurt and abandoned by the body of Christ. This deeply saddens me, as this is not how God intends things to be. God wants each member of the body to feel connected and loved. Why is it that the church is often slow to reach out and minister to those with MCS? I'm sure there are a multitude of reasons, however, I believe the biggest reason is due to ignorance. I think most people are still in the dark when it comes to understanding MCS and how it affects people. Trying to explain MCS to someone who doesn't have it is a bit like trying to explain pregnancy to someone who has never been pregnant. It's a tough job!

In the beginning stages of having MCS, I could still be around fragrances without becoming ill. During that time, a friend of mine with MCS threw a party at her house. She requested that all her friends come "fragrance free." In addition, she went so far as to post a sign on her front door stating that there were no fragrances allowed on those who entered her home. In my ignorance, I recall thinking it was a bit rude of her to ask people not to wear fragrances to her party. I felt she was making too big of a deal out of the fragrance issue. Because this was such a new concept to me, I didn't have a clue as to how sick people could become when exposed to the chemicals in fragrances.

I think once mainstream society becomes more educated about chemical sensitivities, we will begin to see the church becoming more willing to accommodate those with MCS. I Corinthians 12:21–22 gives the body of Christ some insight as to how to treat weaker members. It says this:

The eye cannot say to the hand, "I don't need you!" And the head cannot say to the feet, "I don't need you!" On the contrary, those parts of the body that seem to be weaker and indispensable, and the parts that we think are less honorable we treat with special honor.

Did you hear that? The body of Christ needs the weaker members to function properly, and they should be treated with special honor!

As the leaders in churches slowly become more aware of MCS, we need to give them grace as they begin to understand our illness. One thing that makes MCS so difficult to understand is that each of us reacts to different substances. In addition, the types of symptoms we experience vary from person to person as well. This can be confusing to people as they seek to find ways to make church services and other functions safe for us. We need to be grateful and express appreciation when churches start to take baby steps to accommodate us.

Let's pray that God will help society and the church become more educated on the topic of MCS. Another thing to pray is that the body of Christ will develop a heart of compassion for those with MCS. Lastly, please join me in praying that God will open doors for us to get assimilated back into church activities.

A Goal Worth Striving For

Not that we are competent in ourselves to claim anything for our-selves, but our competence comes from God.

(2 Corinthians 3:5)

$\mathcal{P}$rior to having a chronic illness, I always wanted to appear strong and capable. People often admire those who are highly energetic and accomplish a lot. It is generally not those who are weak physically or emotionally that people look up to. Therefore, many of us spend our lives trying to fit into society's idea of what it means to be a success. Most of my life I felt that if I was not going ninety miles an hour all day, then I was not a worthwhile or productive person. How crazy is that? Can anyone else relate to that self-imposed pressure?

Even though I have made some strides in accepting my limitations and allowing myself time to rest, at times I still find myself feeling wound up. Throughout the day, I may catch myself feeling tense when there is no reason to feel that way. For example, I may find myself brushing my teeth at a furious pace, or when I'm in the shower, sometimes I notice my toes curling under from thinking about what I need to do next in my day. During those times, I have to remind myself to take a deep breath and relax, knowing it is not good for my immune system to be in high gear all the time.

Remember the classic song that many of us sang in Sunday School as children entitled, "Jesus Loves Me?" One of the lines in the song says, "Little ones to Him belong. They are weak, but He is strong." Boy, can I relate to that now! Having a chronic illness has taken away any confidence I used to have in my own abilities or strength. It is refreshing to know that the apostle Paul often boasted about his weakness. Listen to what he has to say: *"If I must boast, I will boast of the things that show my weakness"* (2 Corinthians 11:30).

What should we be striving for in life? One of my favorite verses addresses this very important question. Jeremiah 9:23 says:

> *Let not the wise man boast of his wisdom or the strong man boast of his strength or the rich man boast of his riches, but let him who boasts boast about this: that he understands and knows me.*

Now that's a verse packed full of wisdom! According to this verse, to understand and know God is a goal worth pursuing in life. How do we get to know Him? One way is by reading and meditating on His Word. Another way is by being still before Him and letting Him speak to our hearts and minds. Psalm 1:1–2 says:

> *Blessed is the man who does not walk in the counsel of the wicked or stand in the way of sinners or sit in the seat of mockers. But his delight is in the law of the Lord, and on his law he meditates day and night.*

This week, let's make it our aim to get to know and understand God. That is a goal worth striving for.

Suicide

He came to a broom tree, sat down under it and prayed that he might die. "I have had enough, Lord," he said. "Take my life; I am no better than my ancestors."

(I Kings 19:4)

It is common for those with MCS to go through periods where death seems like an inviting option. According to Molly Jensen, who specializes in counseling people with MCS, most people who are chemically sensitive have thoughts about death or suicide at one time or another. You are not alone if you have struggled with these types of thoughts. If you happen to be thinking about suicide, please don't do it!

At times, when living with MCS, our circumstances may seem too much for us to handle on our own. The good news is that God promises that He will help us through whatever trial we are going through, no matter how deep and painful it is. 2 Corinthians 1:8–9 says:

We were under great pressure, far beyond our ability to endure, so that we despaired even of life. Indeed, in our hearts we felt the sentence of death. But this happened that we might not rely on ourselves but on God, who raises the dead.

During certain seasons of our lives, we may become so overwhelmed that we feel we can't make it another step. When we're in that mindset, we need to rely solely on God to help us. Sometimes He allows us to be pressed beyond our human ability to endure so that we will humble ourselves and cry out to Him, knowing we can't make it through life on our own. Listen to Paul's testimony of how God rescued him from a severe trial:

He has delivered us from such a deadly peril, and he will deliver us. On him we have set our hope that he will continue to deliver us.
(2 Corinthians 1:10)

One day when the challenges I was facing made me question how much longer I could take the pain of life, I told my counselor, Molly, that I wanted to die. Her response to me was that I didn't really want to die—what I wanted was my circumstances to change. That made so much sense to me! When times get tough, giving up on life is not the answer. Suicide is a permanent solution to a temporary problem. The enemy loves to try and get us so discouraged that we lose hope that things will ever improve.

I'm so glad I have persevered through all the trials that MCS has brought into my life. Even though it has not been an easy journey, God has been faithful to sustain me day-by-day, hour-by-hour, and sometimes minute-by-minute. My circumstances have changed so much for the better over the years that I stand in awe of all that God has done for me.

Today, if life seems more than you can bear, reach out to Jesus for help, trusting Him to intervene on your behalf. Persevere through the trials and struggles of MCS. James 1:12 says:

Blessed is the man who perseveres under trial, because when he has stood the test, he will receive the crown of life that God has promised to those who love him.

If you persevere, you will be richly rewarded.

Shallow Roots

Foxes have holes and birds of the air have nests, but the Son of Man has no place to lay his head.

(Matthew 8:20)

*L*ife with MCS is unpredictable. In the summer of 2002, my family went camping to our favorite spot at a Thousand Trails campground. After a fun-filled day of sightseeing, we went back to our RV at 11 P.M., only to find it filled with smoke that had drifted inside from our neighbors' campfires. By that time of night, I was exhausted and ready for bed. Since I had no "safe" place to sleep, I hopped in our truck and drove around for an hour and a half. At 12:30 A.M., I called my husband who assured me it was finally safe to come back.

Many of us have had times when we have been displaced temporarily or permanently from our living spaces that have become tainted. After our home became contaminated from a toxic air freshener, my family stayed with my parents for three months. During our time there, one day a housecleaner came in to clean with ammonia and other chemicals. Since I had two young children and chronic fatigue, it was difficult for me to go places. The closest place I could think of to go hang out for the day was a local library, so I ended up taking my kids there. What a challenge it was to have to go somewhere for the day when I felt sick and exhausted! It was frustrating not only to have my own home unavailable to me, but now I couldn't even find rest in my temporary home.

I know many with MCS have suffered much worse than me. I have talked with numerous people who have had to live in their cars for periods of time. Those of us with MCS often just do what we have to do in order to survive in our toxic society.

Have you gone through a period where you have been displaced or even homeless? Maybe you are currently looking for a "safe" place to live. During my most desperate moments in living with MCS, one verse that has often comforted me is Romans 8:18, which says:

> *I consider that our present sufferings are not worth comparing with the glory that will be revealed in us.*

This verse helps me stay focused on the fact that this world is not my real home, and so I shouldn't let my roots go too deep while on this planet. I need to remind myself that I am just a camper passing through. The apostle Paul was a great example of someone who looked forward to his heavenly home:

> *Therefore we are always confident and know that as long as we are at home in the body we are away from the Lord. We are confident, I say, and would prefer to be away from the body and at home with the Lord.*
>
> (2 Corinthians 5:6,8)

If your living situation on this earth is temporarily or permanently taken away from you, take comfort in the fact that your real home in heaven is waiting for you. Colossians 3:1 says: *"Since, then, you have been raised with Christ, set your hearts on things above, where Christ is seated at the right hand of God."*

Free to Be Me

Better to be lowly in spirit and among the oppressed than to share plunder with the proud.

(Proverbs 16:19)

One thing I've noticed about those of us with MCS is our ability to be real. Many of us have been stripped of the trappings we used to try and impress people with. Our physical appearance may be different than before we became ill since many of us cannot tolerate wearing dry cleaned clothes, dying our hair, or wearing certain types of fabrics. Many of us do not have prestigious titles, careers, or large bank accounts. We may have lost our ability to perform in community service or ministry positions. Without the props that we used to need in order to feel successful in life, we should be free to relax and be ourselves.

Prior to becoming ill, I didn't feel comfortable being totally real with people. I feared if people knew about my struggles and humanity, they might reject me. Fortunately, I no longer feel that way. What a freeing thing it has been not to have to prove anything to anyone! The Bible exhorts us not to think of ourselves more highly than we ought to. Romans 12:3 says:

> *Do not think of yourself more highly than you ought, but rather think of yourself with sober judgment, in accordance with the measure of faith God has given you.*

MCS is quite a humbling experience for most of us. If we allow God to break down the walls of pride in our lives, it can be a very positive thing. Our lives will no longer be consumed with trying to impress others, and we will be free to be the people He created us to be. Having nothing to prove, we can admit our faults and weaknesses openly with others, knowing God is the only one in life we need to please. As we are vulnerable with one another, we can help support each other through the trials of life.

Once we let God deal with pride in our lives, we can have healthier relationships, as we accept people regardless of race, financial status, or physical appearance. We can associate with all types of people and perhaps get to know people we had nothing in common with before we became ill. Hopefully we can embrace people and love them unconditionally as Christ would have us to. Romans 12:16 gives us this exhortation:

> *Do not be proud, but be willing to associate with people of low position. Do not be conceited.*

This week, let's praise God for the freedom we have in Christ to be ourselves, knowing He loves us just the way we are. In turn, let's show that same love to others who come across our paths.

Roller Coaster Ride

The Lord upholds all those who fall and lifts up all who are bowed down.

(Psalm 145:14)

Have you ever had a week where you wonder how many more problems on this earth you can take? Life is hard no matter what a person's circumstances, but somehow adding a chronic illness to the mix can sometimes make life seem too much to bear. I love a song by the group 4 Him called "Ride of Life." It talks about life being like a roller coaster ride, since it has a lot of ups and downs. Isn't that how MCS feels sometimes? Some days for me are really enjoyable, yet other days I may have an exposure where I'm really sick and depressed, begging the Lord to return to take His saints home. Life indeed seems like a roller coaster ride!

Recently, I had one of those weeks where the challenges of life were weighing me down. First, my computer had a virus, causing a lot of excess work for me. In addition, my cat was vomiting for four days, so I had the stress of cleaning that up numerous times a day—not exactly my favorite thing to do! Next, I had to take my sick cat to the vet. Since the waiting room had a toxic air freshener in it, I had to talk to the vet in the parking lot, which is located on a very busy street corner. In doing so, I became quite ill from the exhaust I was exposed to. The following day when I was downstairs doing laundry, a propane truck drove up and started filling my neighbor's tank. Before I knew what was happening, the toxic fumes had drifted in my upstairs window. At that point I thought, *Lord, what next? How much more can I take?*

When we become ill from chemical exposures on top of the normal problems in life, it's easy to become discouraged. In Judges 6, Gideon seemed overwhelmed with the circumstances in his life. Listen to a conversation he had with the Lord and an angel who visited him:

> When the angel of the Lord appeared to Gideon, he said, "The Lord is with you, mighty warrior." "But sir," Gideon replied, "if the Lord is with us, why has all this happened to us? Where are all his wonders that our fathers told us about when they said, 'Did not the Lord bring us up out of Egypt?' But now the Lord has abandoned us and put us into the hand of Midian." The Lord turned to him and said, "Go in the strength you have and save Israel out of Midian's hand. Am I not sending you?"
>
> (Judges 6:12–14)

In the midst of his challenges, both the Lord and the angel assured Gideon that God would be with him to help him fight his battles. Psalm 34:19 says: *"A righteous man may have many troubles, but the Lord delivers him from them all."*

When you become weighed down by the pressures of life, try and tell yourself, *Okay, I can make it through one more week through*

Christ's strength. Psalm 55:22 says: *"Cast your cares on the Lord and he will sustain you; he will never let the righteous fall."* The next time life seems like a steep mountain, cast your cares on the Lord and He will sustain you.

New Age or New Life?

I am the way and the truth and the life. No one comes to the Father except through me.

(John 14:6)

For fourteen years, Linda Nathan searched desperately to find meaning and purpose in life. In her quest for freedom, she explored everything from LSD to Eastern religions and white witchcraft. Eventually she became a psychic healer and channeler. However, all her dabbling in various religions and philosophies proved empty. A turning point for Linda came in 1976 when she was diagnosed with cancer. At the end of her rope, Linda had an encounter with the one, true living God. A minister had given her a booklet talking about the healing power of Jesus. That day she met Jesus Christ and found salvation and hope for eternal life through a relationship with Him. The Lord healed Linda from cancer, and she was freed from the delusions and bondage she had been under for so many years.

Today there are many others like Linda who are looking for truth, and, sadly, many are looking in all the wrong places. The New Age Movement has become very popular in today's society, and I think one reason many are attracted to it is because it demands no personal responsibility from its followers. People are encouraged to pursue their own paths in discovering what is right or wrong; there are no moral absolutes. Contender Ministries describes the New Age Movement as "a collection of eastern-influenced metaphysical ideologies, a hodge-podge of theologies and philosophies that are bound together by 'universal tolerance' and 'moral relativism.'"[32]

What's happening today is nothing new. All throughout history, people have been guilty of making up their own religions and belief systems. Some refer to this as "syncretism." According to Doug Goins, "The sin of syncretism is blending loyalties to several gods, mixing and matching religions in a sort of smorgasbord."[33] We see this happening in Israel in the book of Judges where it states: *"Everyone did what was right in his own eyes"* (Judges 21:25 NASB). The problem with this behavior is that God is a jealous God and He will not share His glory with anyone. Exodus 20:3 says: *"You shall have no other gods before me."* The one, true God of the Bible demands allegiance to Him alone.

As we look at the history of Israel, we can learn a lot from the mistakes they made and their pattern of wandering away from Jehovah, the one true God, to serve other gods and goddesses such as Baal and Ashtoreth. Every time Israel would turn to serving other gods, God would remove His hand of blessing from them. After awhile they would repent as we see happening in I Samuel 7:4: *"So the Israelites put away their Baals and Ashtoreths, and served the Lord only."*

Today, if you have not yet found salvation in the one, true God of the universe, I encourage you to do as the Israelites did and put away all other gods and philosophies. Submit your life to Christ today as Lord and Savior. You won't regret it!

The Positive Thinking Trap

Many are the plans in a man's heart, but it is the Lord's purpose that prevails.

(Proverbs 19:21)

Have you ever heard anyone claim that if you just think positive you can control your circumstances? We live in a society that talks a lot about positive thinking. Bookstore shelves are lined with books discussing this concept. Typically, the idea many authors seem to present is that if you have a positive attitude, you can achieve most anything in life you set your heart on. The theory seems to be that if you just work hard enough and believe you will succeed, your dreams will come true.

Now don't get me wrong—positive thinking, in and of itself, is not a bad thing. For the most part, I believe having positive thoughts is a good goal to strive for. However, the danger comes in when people believe that they can control their destiny through it. When people rely solely on positive thinking to achieve desired results in their lives, they are leaving God's sovereignty out of the equation. Those of us who have had a chronic illness for a while know that all the positive thinking in the world will not make us well, nor will it allow us to be able to be around chemical exposures without becoming ill.

After first becoming aware that I had MCS, I went through a period where I made some very poor choices concerning what chemicals I allowed myself to be exposed to. Following the situation where a toxic air freshener had been applied to the carpets in my home, I made the decision to have the old carpets ripped out and replaced with brand new carpeting. At the time, it seemed like the quickest and easiest solution to the problem of tainted carpets. Once the new carpets had been installed, however, I was nervous about testing them, as I knew there was a possibility I could have a reaction to them. A well-intentioned relative had a "positive thinking" type of mentality. He convinced me that if I just had a positive attitude, the carpets would not make me sick. As it turned out, having a positive attitude did not make the brand new carpet "safe" for me; I ended up having a bad reaction.

When making decisions while living with MCS, more than just positive thinking is needed. We need to rely on God's guidance in our lives, realizing He has the ability to control our circumstances. Proverbs 3:5–6 says:

> *Trust in the Lord with all your heart and lean not on your own understanding; in all your ways acknowledge him, and he will make your paths straight.*

Whatever situation in life you may be facing today, pray about what direction God would have you take. Don't rely on positive thinking, but have faith in the God of the universe. If you follow His lead, He will help you fulfill His plan for your life.

The Most Difficult Time of the Year

Today in the town of David a Savior has been born to you; he is Christ the Lord.

(Luke 2:11)

During the Christmas holiday season, there are often expectations that it should be the best time of the year. The reality for a lot of people, however, is that it is a very difficult time. Those with a chronic illness like MCS may think the words to the song "It's the Most Wonderful Time of the Year" should be "It's the Most Difficult Time of the Year." Many of us are no longer able to attend Christmas concerts or parties, go shopping at the mall, or participate in other festivities. For some it can be a very lonely and depressing time. How can we make the holiday season special in the midst of the challenges of MCS?

First, I think it is important to give ourselves permission to grieve. Throughout the Psalms, David shows us by example how to pour out our hearts to God. Listen to David's heartfelt cries during a time of distress:

> *I cry aloud to the Lord; I lift up my voice to the Lord for mercy. I pour out my complaint before him; before him I tell my trouble. When my spirit grows faint within me, it is you who know my way.*
> (Psalm 142:1–3)

Sometimes it helps to express our true feelings, asking the Lord to help us through our difficulties.

Changing our expectations can also help us navigate successfully through the holidays. Think of new ways to enjoy the season such as cooking yourself a special meal at home, enjoying a Christmas concert on television, or decorating your living space with some non-toxic decorations.

Another thing that helps me get through the holidays is to get my eyes off myself and look for ways to bless others. One verse my mother often quoted to me growing up was: *"It is more blessed to give than to receive"* (Acts 20:35). I have found this principle to hold true in my own life—giving to others is a pretty sure way to lift your spirits. Be creative in thinking of simple ways you can give to others. A few ideas would be to send out a Christmas letter to a few relatives and friends, call someone else with MCS that you know may be feeling isolated during the holidays, or donate money to your favorite ministry or charity.

Lastly, during the holidays I recommend spending time alone with God, worshipping Him and thanking Him for the gift of His son, Jesus. Luke 2:13 says: *"Glory to God in the highest, and on earth peace to men on whom his favor rests."* Meditate on what an awesome gift it was for God to send His only son to earth to be born, and to ultimately die for our sins so that we can spend eternity with Him. He is the reason for the season, and it is only right that we give Him the glory due His name.

A New Reality

Whoever loves money never has money enough; whoever loves wealth is never satisfied with his income.

(Ecclesiastes 5:10)

One thing that has helped me to cope with all the losses that MCS has brought into my life is to realize that many of our expectations come from the time period and culture we live in. Back in the pioneer days, life was much different. There were no symphonies to attend, trips to the Caribbean to look forward to, or fancy malls to shop in; life was quite simple. I would guess that if people who lived in that era had food, shelter, and clothing they counted themselves blessed. Today, however, the media shouts messages at us that in order to be happy we need to acquire things. Many people work hard in an effort to achieve a certain lifestyle they think will bring them peace and contentment.

Chuck Swindoll, in his book *Intimacy with the Almighty*, talks about the fast-paced, consumptive society in which we live. He suggests that if we truly want to achieve intimacy with God, we need to simplify our lives. He encourages people to reorder their private worlds, and he feels that "the need to simplify is imperative."[34] Since this concept goes against the grain in our culture, Chuck also makes this profound statement: "Those who determine to simplify their lives quickly discover it is a rigorous solo voyage against the wind."[35]

If we are to live successfully with MCS, I think it is important for us to revamp our thinking; we need to define a new reality for ourselves. As we do this, we can experience contentment in our lives. At times, I have had healthy people express envy toward me due to the simplicity of my life. As they rush to and fro, stressed out in their lives, they see a calmness in me that comes from not having to be constantly on the run. On the flip side of the coin, those of us who are homebound much of the time may be tempted to be envious of those who are out living a hurried lifestyle. We need to guard against that, as a busy life, in and of itself, certainly doesn't bring happiness.

In today's society, we have made life so complicated, and yet Ecclesiastes 12:13 says: *"Fear God and keep his commandments, for this is the whole duty of man."* Doesn't that boil life down to the basics?

As we adjust to the various changes brought about by having MCS, let's seek to simplify our lives. I think as we re-examine our goals and priorities, we will be pleasantly surprised that living a simple life is a happy life. As we define a new reality for ourselves, we will have time to seek God's face and develop an intimacy with Him that busy people often don't have time for. I love Psalm 84:10, which says: *"Better is one day in your courts than a thousand elsewhere."*

Today, let's embrace our simple lives and enjoy spending time in His presence. That is the best reality imaginable!

Flexibility

You ought to say, "If it is the Lord's will, we will live and do this or that."

(James 4:15)

Flexibility is something I have found to be vital in living with MCS successfully. Since we often don't know what to expect when we venture outside our homes in terms of possible chemical exposures, it is prudent to have Plans "A, B, C, and D" ready in case our initial plans don't work out. Traveling is one thing that often requires numerous back-up plans. Because the risks of traveling can be great, for five years I didn't travel more than an hour or two from home. In the spring of 2003, however, I felt a bit more adventuresome, so I planned a trip to the ocean with my family, which is about a four-hour drive from where I live.

The night before our departure, I called my friend, Lori, as I started becoming a bit nervous about this adventure. *What would I do if my family drove for four hours only to find out the hotel we booked was toxic to me?* I started wondering if I was making a mistake by planning this trip. Lori and I brainstormed together and came up with multiple plans in case the hotel room was too toxic for me. Plan "A" was for me to sleep by an open window or door. Plan "B" was to get a rollaway bed and have me sleep on the deck under the stars. I wasn't sure how practical that idea was, however, since the Washington coast is not known for its warm temperatures! Plan "C" was to look for another room in a nearby town. If all else failed, Plan "D" was to turn around and drive home.

The day of our trip, my family set out at eleven o'clock in the morning. The weather was sunny and the traffic wasn't too heavy considering it was a holiday weekend. We stopped for lunch at a restaurant on the way to the ocean. As we neared our destination, I started becoming apprehensive again about what would happen if the hotel room didn't work for me. In the midst of my fears, I thought of Proverbs 2:7, which says: *"He holds victory in store for the upright."* I felt this might be the Lord's confirmation to me that all would go well.

Once we got to our hotel, we checked out our room that had been specially cleaned by the housekeeping staff with vinegar, and it worked great for me! I was so thankful to the Lord for making this dream come true. I had so desired to have a family vacation at the ocean that my kids would remember. They had the time of their lives cramming a lot of activities into two days. They went horseback riding, rode mopeds and go-carts, went swimming, and played on the beach. These will be memories my family will always cherish.

Plans don't always work out as we anticipate, but if we entrust our lives to the Heavenly Father, He will be with us and help us no matter what happens. Whatever plans you may have for your future, place them in God's hands, asking Him to be with you and to guide you. Psalm 52:8 says: *"I trust in God's unfailing love for ever and ever."* He will never let us down!

Embrace the Fire

For our "God is a consuming fire."

(Hebrews 12:29)

Harry and Cheryl Salem lived through every parent's nightmare—the death of a child. Their beautiful, five-year-old daughter, Gabrielle, was diagnosed with an inoperable brain tumor. After eleven months of battling her illness, Gabrielle went home to be with Jesus. The year after her home going, Cheryl was diagnosed with colon cancer. She was so distraught with grief over her daughter's death that she secretly hoped the cancer would be her escape from the trial. *Perhaps if the cancer kills me, I could go home to be with Gabrielle,* she thought. Over the next few years, God did some amazing things in Harry and Cheryl's hearts through the fire of affliction. They now minister to others in difficult circumstances as they share the testimony of healing and restoration in their lives. The Salems have written two books, *From Mourning to Morning* and *From Grief to Glory,* that specifically deal with the issues of grief and loss.

What is your response when God allows trials to come your way? Do you desperately wish to escape from them? Do you experience emotions such as guilt or anger? Do you find yourself depressed and barely able to cope? These are all very common responses, and I have experienced every one of them. Recently though, I have felt the Lord impress upon me a better way of dealing with the difficulties of life. The words that keep coming to mind are *Embrace the fire.* Rather than try and run from the fire of affliction, I feel the Lord is telling me I need to wake up each morning with the attitude that I will embrace it. You may be wondering, *Why on earth would I want to embrace the fire of affliction?* Hebrews 12:11 gives some insight on this question:

> *No discipline seems pleasant at the time, but painful. Later on, however, it produces a harvest of righteousness and peace for those who have been trained by it.*

You see, when we go through difficulties, it can be God's way of disciplining us and training us to be more like Him. As hard as it is to go through the fires of affliction, if we let God do His work in our hearts, they will "produce a harvest of righteousness" in our lives. Who wouldn't want that?

I love the story in the Old Testament about Shadrach, Meshach, and Abednego. King Nebuchadnezzar had these three men tied up and thrown into a blazing furnace for refusing to worship a gold image that he had set up in Babylon. The fire was so hot that the flames killed the soldiers who were ordered to throw the men in. Once the men were in the furnace, the King was astounded when he saw them walking around. In Daniel 3:25, King Nebuchadnezzar said:

"Look! I see four men walking around in the fire, unbound and un-harmed, and the fourth looks like a son of the gods."

After seeing this, the King had the men come out of the fur-nace. Look what happened next:

And the satraps, prefects, governors and royal advisers crowded around them. They saw that the fire had not harmed their bodies, nor was a hair of their heads singed; their robes were not scorched, and there was no smell of fire on them.

(Daniel 3:27)

Shadrach, Meshach, and Abednego lived through the fiery fur-nace because God was with them.

When we are going through challenges in our lives, no matter how "hot" the fire gets, the trial will not destroy us if we trust the Lord to bring us through. Today, let's be willing to "embrace the fires" in our lives, knowing they will produce a harvest of righ-teousness if we let them.

Stages of Grief

O Lord, hear my prayer, listen to my cry for mercy; in your faithfulness and righteousness come to my relief.

(Psalm 143:1)

Grieving is a part of life. Those of us with MCS are not coping with the physical death of a person, but we are dealing with the death of our dreams. The manner in which we grieve can be similar to what people experience when a loved one dies. Everyone grieves differently, but some of the stages I have passed through as I have dealt with MCS include denial, anger, and acceptance. In living with MCS, I continue to go in and out of some of these stages as I encounter new chemical exposures and other challenges along the path of life.

Denial is the first stage I went through as the warning signs of MCS started appearing. When I had my first crisis with MCS symptoms, I figured it was just a temporary problem that could be solved; I thought I would get over it. After all, I'd always been a very active person who was involved in a lot of activities. When I became ill from toxic oil paint that had been applied to the condo my family was living in, I figured we'd just find another place to live and my life would be normal again. Boy, was I wrong about that!

During the early phases of MCS, I kept pressing on, trying to ignore my body's warning signs that something was amiss. I pushed myself through the pain and symptoms until I eventually collapsed. It was then that I was forced to face the reality that I had a chronic illness. At this stage I experienced anger—anger that many aspects of my life had been stripped away, and I wondered how I was going to cope with the monumental losses before me.

Job knew firsthand about losses. In one fell swoop, all of his children died in a windstorm. In addition, he lost most of his servants and animals due to various catastrophes. If that wasn't enough, God allowed Job to be afflicted with painful sores all over his body from head to toe. At that point in his life, Job appeared to be frustrated. In questioning God, he said this: "*If I have sinned, what have I done to you, O watcher of men? Why have you made me your target?*" (Job 7:20) God can handle our honesty when we are frustrated or angry. He loves us and accepts us no matter what phase of grieving we may be in.

Having gone through various emotions through the years while grieving, I now make it my goal to accept my circumstances, regardless of whether or not God chooses to heal me. Whatever assignments God may have for me in the midst of my challenges, I strive to face them with an attitude of joy and contentment. King David's life exemplifies the attitude God wants us to have. Acts 13:22 says: "*I have found David son of Jesse a man after my own heart; he will do everything I want him to do.*"

Whatever emotions in the grieving process you may be experiencing right now, I encourage you to make it a goal to move towards the acceptance of your present situation. There you will find joy and contentment.

The Party Never Ends

A cheerful heart is good medicine, but a crushed spirit dries up the bones.

(Proverbs 17:22)

A friend of mine, Johanna Wolf, has taught me a lot about the importance of maintaining a sense of humor in the midst of the trials of MCS. Johanna was one of the first people I met after discovering I was chemically sensitive. I met her in a local support group, and I'm so glad I did! The early years of MCS were a very uncertain and frightening time for me. I was having bizarre reactions to toxic chemicals, and I wasn't sure how to make it through those scary episodes. When I would become disoriented from chemical exposures, I would often call Johanna, who with her bright sense of humor made it much easier for me to cope. She always had a funny comment to lift my spirits. One of her classic lines that always gave me a chuckle was, "The party never ends!"

The Bible has some good advice concerning the importance of our emotional wellbeing and its impact on our physical health.

Proverbs 18:14 says: *"A man's spirit sustains him in sickness, but a crushed spirit who can bear?"* This verse seems to indicate that our emotional state can help sustain us during times of illness. When we are really sick, it's not always easy to stay positive, but anything we can do to keep our spirits up as much as possible can be beneficial to our health. A good sense of humor can certainly make our dark days brighter.

Part of Johanna's sense of humor includes having fun playing tricks on people. On numerous occasions, Johanna has called me, disguising her voice like a man and informing me that she is a pesticide applicator planning to spray next door that day. At times I momentarily believed her, and then when I found out it was she, we had a good laugh together. I have been known to play the trick back on Johanna and on others with MCS as well.

Another person in my life that has blessed me with her sense of humor is my daughter, Brittany. Ever since she was born, she has always been the life of the party. Even as a baby, people would comment on Brittany's fun-loving personality. She enjoys joke books and gets a kick out of pulling pranks on people. Not surprisingly, one of her favorite holidays is April Fools' Day! Brittany has a Sanguine personality type in contrast to my Melancholy personality type. Those of us with a Melancholy personality type are generally more serious by nature, and can often benefit from the Sanguines around us who are known for their optimism, bubbling personalities, and sense of humor.[36] I thank God for my precious daughter, Brittany, who has brought so much joy to my life through her animated personality.

Whatever you may be experiencing today in your life because of MCS, try to find some humor in the midst of the challenges. If this doesn't come natural for you, ask the Lord to help you develop a more light-hearted spirit in your life.

Physical Healing

Heal me, O Lord, and I will be healed; save me and I will be saved, for you are the one I praise.

(Jeremiah 17:14)

People often ask me how I went from being bedridden sixteen to twenty hours per day six years ago to living a semi-active lifestyle now. I still have MCS and continue to have to be very careful about where I go, but I am no longer a shut-in like I once was. Before I discuss this topic, I'd like to point out that there are no magic bullets that work for improving MCS. There are still so many unknowns about the condition. Everyone has different systems that appear to be damaged either temporarily or permanently, so the treatments that help one person may not help another. Also, I'd like to make it clear that some people may get over MCS completely, while others receive partial or no healing. Ultimately, God is in control of each of our lives. Those things being said, I'd like to share a few of the things that I feel have contributed to the positive changes in my health.

First of all, I give God the glory and credit for any improvement in my health. James 1:17 says: *"Every good and perfect gift is from above, coming down from the Father of the heavenly lights, who does not change like shifting shadows."* I have had a lot of people pray for me over the years, so that is the first thing I believe has helped me. Beyond that, there are some other things I feel have helped as well. As far as medical treatments go, I have taken a variety of vitamins and supplements over the years that have helped build my immune system. In addition, I have taken homeopathic remedies and other products to help overcome food allergies and Candida. Having my mercury amalgams out was also a positive experience for me, as I noticed an increase of energy and a lessening of my chemical sensitivities following their removal.

As far as my emotional life is concerned, I feel that hope has been a key factor in the improvement of my health. Proverbs 13:12 says: *"Hope deferred makes the heart sick, but a longing fulfilled is a tree of life."* Back when I was homebound most of the time, I became pretty hopeless. Since I was only able to leave my home occasionally without becoming ill from chemical exposures, I felt very isolated and alone. Life seemed to be passing me by. That all changed, however, when my precious sister, Pam, reached out and helped restore my hope. In the spring of 2001, my family went to Disneyland without me, as I was too ill to go. Knowing this was a sad time for me, my sister Pam came and spent the week with me. That simple gesture meant the world to me, and I will be forever grateful for her sacrifice. Her kindness assured me that I would not be stuck in isolation forever. There were still people who loved and cared about me.

Lastly, I think my overall health has improved as I have allowed the Lord to use His pruning shears to lop off those branches in me that weren't bearing fruit. John 15:1–2 says:

I am the true vine, and my Father is the gardener. He cuts off every branch in me that bears no fruit, while every branch that does bear fruit he prunes so that it will be even more fruitful.

Through the years, the Lord has helped me deal with sins in my life such as selfishness, codependency, and many more. Psalm 51:17 says: *"The sacrifices of God are a broken spirit; a broken and contrite heart, O God, you will not despise."* God will honor our prayers when we confess our sins and ask Him to make us pure and holy.

Today, I encourage you to ask God to lead you to the answers for healing in your own life. Ask Him to direct you to the right doctors and medical treatments, as well as to show you areas of your emotional and spiritual life that need healing. Psalm 51:6 says: *"Surely you desire truth in the inner parts; you teach me wisdom in the inmost place."* May the Lord bless you in your journey toward better health, knowing we will all be healed someday whether it's on this earth or in the life to come!

Epilogue

*T*he rich spiritual lessons I've learned through having MCS have been well worth the pain and suffering associated with this illness. I have much more peace in my life now than before I had this condition. Yes, there are still great challenges and times of discouragement, but there is a peace that passes understanding that comes from viewing suffering from God's perspective. There is a contentment that comes from trusting in God's sovereignty, and knowing His plans for my life are best.

The biggest impact MCS has had on my life is to help me realize that this world is not my real home; it is only a temporary residence. It has helped me release my grip on things of this earth and look forward to my home in heaven. It has helped diminish the pain of this life, as I anticipate being a co-heir with Christ someday. One thing that gives me great joy and hope is imagining all believers throughout the ages gathered in heaven worshipping the Lamb of God on His throne. What a glorious experience that will be! I Corinthians 2:9 says: *"No eye has seen, no ear has heard, no mind has conceived what God has prepared for those who love him."* We can't begin to comprehend the joys and pleasures that await us in heaven.

If you haven't yet committed your life to Christ, I would like to share with you how to accept his free gift of eternal life. In doing so, you, too, can look forward to eternity in heaven. It's very simple. Just talk to God like you would a friend. Tell Him you'd like to accept His free gift of salvation. Admit you are a sinner and that you need His power in your life to make you like Him.

Once you do this, it's important to spend time in God's Word to get to know Him. You can either read the Bible, or listen to it on CDs or cassettes. There are also a lot of good Bible teachers that can be heard on the radio or Internet. I recommend *The Word for Today*, which is a radio ministry sponsored by Calvary Chapel in Costa Mesa, California: *www.thewordfortoday.org*. At this Web site you will find a daily radio message by Pastor Chuck Smith. In addition, there are archives of other sermons by Chuck Smith, Jon Courson, Don McClure, and other excellent Bible teachers.

If you are able to attend church, it is a great way to get to know other believers. There are a lot of good Bible-believing churches around the country. If you are interested in finding a Calvary Chapel in your area, a list of churches nationwide can be found at: *www.calvarychapel.org*. In the various Calvary Chapel churches I've attended, people typically dress quite casually, and the perfume level often seems to be lower than in the average church.

Chuck Smith, the founder of the Calvary Chapel movement, is well known for ministering to the hippies in the '60s, who were considered by many to be society's outcasts. Calvary Eastside is following his example by reaching out to the afflicted with MCS who often don't feel valued by society. In addition to providing a Fragrance Free Zone for the chemically sensitive on Sunday mornings, the church welcomes those with MCS to participate in their outdoor picnics and baptisms. They also put notices periodically in their church bulletins asking people to refrain from wearing fragrances to services. I hope that in coming years many other churches will learn how to reach out to those with MCS. It is my dream that many who have been unable to attend services due to their sensitivities will be able to re-enter church life. I know the Lord will bless churches that will be willing to accommodate the chemically sensitive. Isaiah 58:10 says:

> And if you spend yourselves in behalf of the hungry and satisfy the needs of the oppressed, then your light will rise in the darkness, and your night will become like the noonday.

May the Lord richly bless all of you as you continue on your journeys with MCS. I hope to see you in heaven where there will be no more sickness, no more pain, and no more MCS. What a grand party we will have!

In Christ's love,
Janine

Notes

1. The Rock Church. Go to the "Mission to Mexico" link. (*http://www.therockchurch.info/outreach/mexico.html*).
2. The interview by Hank Hanegraaff on Christian Research Institute's radio program the *Bible Answer Man* took place on May 2, 1995. For further information on the interview, contact CRI at 1 (888) 7000-CRI.
3. C.L Barnhart, Editor in Chief, *The American College Dictionary* (New York: Random House, 1966), 515.
4. Everett F. Harrison, Editor, *The Wycliffe Bible Commentary* (Chicago: Moody Press, 1962), 1445.
5. Charles Caldwell Ryrie, *The Ryrie Study Bible* (Chicago: Moody Press, 1978), 1114.
6. Colin Nickerson, "The Smell Test: Halifax stirs emotions with ban on scents," *Boston Globe,* May 26, 2000, A01.
7. I got this information from the video: *Wings of the Morning,* School of Tomorrow, P.O. Box 1438 Lewisville, TX 75067, (214) 315–1776.
8. Wholesome Words. Go to the "Biographies" link where you will find *The Works of Jonathan Edwards*: Mr. Brainerd's Remains. Consisting of Letters and Other Papers. (*http://www.wholesomewords.org*).
9. Ibid.

10. Ibid.
11. Charles Caldwell Ryrie, *The Ryrie Study Bible* (Chicago: Moody Press, 1978), 710.
12. Elisabeth Elliot, *A Path Through Suffering* (Michigan: Servant Publications, 1990), 188.
13. Dr. V. Gilbert Beers and Ronald A. Beers, General Editors, *TouchPoint Bible* (Wheaton: Tyndale House Publishers, Inc., 1996), 1176.
14. Everett F. Harrison, Editor, *The Wycliffe Bible Commentary* (Chicago: Moody Press, 1962), 1493.
15. Charlie Finch with Dr. Jack Hinze, Pharm.D., NMD, Sharon Finch, Karen Stene Finch, *We Won't Let You Die!,* (Duck River Publishing, 1995), 168.
16. Corrie Ten Boom Museum, "The Hiding Place," (*http://www.corrietenboom.com/history.htm*).
17. Charles R. Swindoll, *Intimacy with the Almighty* (J. Countryman, 1999), 26.
18. I got some of the ideas in this paragraph from Chuck Swindoll's book, *Intimacy with the Almighty*, (J. Countryman, 1999).
19. C.L. Barnhart, Editor in Chief, *The American College Dictionary* (New York: Random House, 1966), 322.
20. I got this idea from the "Daring to Dream Again" 50-day adventure journal. To get a copy of the inspiring journal, call Mainstay at 1 (800) 224–2735, or visit: (*http://www.teamsundays.org*).
21. I got several facts from this paragraph from the following Web site: The Cindy Duehring MCS Research Fund, (*http://ciin.org/fund.htm*). To donate to this fund, contact: P.O. Box 301 White Sulphur Springs, MT 59645. (406) 547–2255.
22. C.L. Barnhart, Editor in Chief, *The American College Dictionary* (New York: Random House, 1966), 478.
23. June Hunt, *Healing the Hurting Heart* (Eugene, Oregon: Harvest House Publishers, 1995), 56.
24. Ibid.
25. Gary Thomas, *Sacred Marriage* (Grand Rapids, Michigan: Zondervan, 2000), 75.
26. Roever and Associates: (*http://www.daveroever.net/index.html*).
27. Chuck Smith, *Why Grace Changes Everything* (Santa Ana, California: The Word for Today, 1994), 13.
28. Some of the information from this devotional was taken from an audio cassette by Jon Courson entitled, *Tests in Life*. Copies may

be obtained through: Firefighters for Christ, 10928 40th Ave. E., Tacoma, WA 98466.

29. I got this idea from Jon Courson's tape *Tests in Life.*

30. Bruce Wilkinson, *The Prayer of Jabez* (Sisters, Oregon: Multnomah Publishers, Inc., 2000), 41.

31. Contender Ministries: "New Age," (*http:// www.contenderministries.org*).

32. Doug Goins, *The Sin of Syncretism,* (*http://www.pbc.org/dp/goins*).

33. Charles R. Swindoll, *Intimacy with the Almighty* (J. Countryman, 1999), 28.

34. Ibid, 30.

35. Florence & Marita Littauer, *Getting Along with Almost Anybody* (Grand Rapids, Michigan: Fleming H. Revell—a division of Baker Book House Co., 1998), 336.

To order additional copies of

COMFORT
in the
STORM

Have your credit card ready and call:

1-877-421-READ (7323)

or please visit our Web site at
www.pleasantword.com

Also available at:
www.amazon.com
and
www.barnesandnoble.com

Printed in the United States
48954LVS00004B/25

9 781414 101408